Help!
I'm Turning Into
My Mother

BECKY FREEMAN
& RUTHIE ARNOLD

HARVEST HOUSE™ PUBLISHERS

EUGENE, OREGON

Published in association with the literary agency of Alive Communications Inc., 7680 Goddard St., Suite 200, Colorado Springs, CO 80920.

Cover by Koechel Peterson & Associates, Minneapolis, Minnesota

HELP! I'M TURNING INTO MY MOTHER
Some of the material in this book is taken from *Adult Children of Fairly Functional Parents*
Copyright © 2002 by Becky Freeman and Ruthie Arnold
Published by Harvest House Publishers
Eugene, Oregon 97402

ISBN 0-7394-2872-1

*To Rachel Praise, our daughter and granddaughter,
as we watch her turn from little girl into beautiful bride.*

Acknowledgments

With enormous gratitude to the people at Harvest House, who treat their authors like friends and family. Each of you has helped make this book a pleasure to produce.

Greg Johnson is not only Becky's agent, but a beloved brother. May all who read this book find a friend and professional partner as good as he.

Thank you to Rachel (Ruthie's younger daughter, Becky's sister) for her fun sense of humor and ever-ready input as we put this book together. Kudos to George (Ruthie's husband, Becky's father) for his patient reading of the manuscript—and for laughing or tearing up at all the right places.

Contents

∿

∿

Prelude:
A Pair of
Chocolate Nuts

A Pair of Chocolate Nuts

~

They sit on our shoulders and whisper in our ears, even when they're a thousand miles away. At times you can't live with 'em, but there are also moments when it seems you can't possibly live without 'em. The best of them hurt us now and then, but even the worst of them manage to come through for us occasionally. How do we escape from the Omnipresent Mother?

Lately, I've been noticing an interesting phenomenon. My mother is taking over my physical body. I never thought it would happen to *moi*. Mother's calluses have appeared on my heels, and her varicose veins adorn my calves, the result of some proud maternal gene with a unique sense of exterior design. (As an aside, when I ran this chapter through the spell check, it suggested I replace "varicose" with "fricassee." This is a true story.)

This morning I happened to glance in the mirror, and I saw that my lipstick had run into tiny new indentations around my lips. I thought for a startled moment that I saw Mother's knowing twinkle reflected back at me. When I told her about it, she seemed totally unsurprised.

"I wish I could tell you there'll never be another shock like that, but the pace is guaranteed to pick up, my dear. As a matter of fact, I had a similar experience just last week. I had washed my hair in the kitchen and wrapped an old towel around my head. In the bathroom, I glanced in the mirror at the towel-draped lady staring back at me.

"My goodness," I said to the lady in the reflection, "you're not only beginning to look like your mother—you're beginning to look like Mother Teresa!"

"So," I said, "there's no end to it?"

"Not in this life!" Mother Ruthie laughed.

Besides the eerie "I'm Turning into My Mother" episodes I've been experiencing of late, I often wonder just how many times today's liberated women from all across this nation secretly find themselves needing to make a decision of grave importance—such as whether to buy one-ply or two-ply tissue—and then asking themselves, *I wonder what Mom would do?*

In many ways I am like my mother. We laugh at the same things, enjoy lingering over lunch at the cafeteria, chat about the trivial, and philosophize over the meaning of life. We both cry over romantic movies, triumphant chorales, and the emotional moments when we finally find our cars in crowded mall parking lots. However, the older I get, the more I realize that, though I am definitely my mother's daughter, I am not her clone. I have made my Declaration of Independence.

Some years ago when the two of us were moving through the line at a cafeteria, I brazenly overlooked the gooey fudge desserts and reached for a bowl of plain egg custard. Mother stopped and placed her hand over her heart as she struggled to recover from this moment of betrayal.

"We don't like egg custard in our family," she finally managed to say. "It's bland. It's plain. It tastes like scrambled eggs with sugar in it. It's for dull people with ulcerated stomachs. We are strong, chocolate-nut women!"

How could I argue with that? But since I had come this far out of the Plain-Vanilla closet, I charged ahead recklessly. "Mother"—I swallowed hard—"I've been wanting to tell you this for a long time. Please try to understand. You were bound to find out, so I might as well be the one to tell you. I also like...tapioca pudding."

Bewilderment clouded her eyes. But, though taken aback, Mother has always tried hard to be a "with-it" kind of mom, wanting to support us in all of our decisions. Eventually she even joined me in sharing a bowl of bread pudding. So she smothered her half with caramel sauce. It's the gesture that counts.

That day we began to talk about the gradual but profound changes that had been taking place in our relationship over a period of time without either of us really realizing it. We had clearly, and sometimes painfully, moved from a relationship that was primarily "mother and daughter" to one of being good buddies.

"Sounds like there's a book in there somewhere," I mused.

"Sure would help if at least one of us was an authority," she sighed.

We decided not to let that tiny deficit hold us back. We'd write the book anyway. Surely somebody out there would be interested in reading a book by two survivors of a Major Passage in Life, amateurs though we might be.

"I've been around a long time," Mother said, "and you know lots of people. We might expand it to include other Passages that have to be navigated! We could even make use of the wreckage!" Not one to waste anything, she was becoming excited.

When my relationship with my mother expanded to include professional writing, my confidence in my own judgment and ability began to increase. But I wasn't sure my mother had made the complete transition. I remember a day when we had been on the phone, making a date for our next meeting at the cafeteria.

"It's going to be raining," she said before signing off. "You'll need a raincoat, you know. Oh, dear," she said, "there I go again." My heart skipped a beat, but then she added, "Oh, well. I might as well say it. Don't forget to go potty before you leave."

Obviously, this Mother/Friend/Equal idea was going to require a little reinforcement, I decided, and today was as good a time as any. I seized the opportunity to assert myself once more. We were finishing our spinach salads when the waitress walked by pushing the beverage cart.

"May I get you anything? A cup of coffee, perhaps?" she inquired. I waited until I was sure I had mother's full attention, and then I spoke with deliberate casualness.

"Yes, I'd like a cup, please." From the corner of my eye, I saw Mother sit straighter in her chair, as if she had been poked in the back by an invisible finger.

"You don't drink coffee!" she said in amazement. "You don't even like it!"

"I know," I replied in my most professional co-writer sort of voice. "I'm making a unilateral decision to enjoy some anyway. I relish holding the cup and savoring the aroma. It makes me look quite sophisticated, don't you think?"

Since we had by this time committed ourselves to writing a book based in part on how successful Mother had been in allowing her daughter to be her own person, she swallowed hard before answering, "Come to think of it, it does!" Then she smiled a wicked smile, lifted her own cup to mine in a toast, and said, "Don't spill it."

It was fun, that moment of wanton rebellion…that flaunting of my radical independence from all my mother thinks I am. As I sipped my coffee (which tasted an awful lot like warm turpentine), my mind drifted to a mental image of a large and flourishing Family Tree. I was obviously on the road to being in emotional control of my own life, but had I yet truly discovered and feathered my own nest, so to speak, on a branch of our tree? Maybe through the process of writing this book with my mom, I'd discover my unique roost among its leafy boughs.

Basically, Mother and I decided to venture out on a limb and explore our own relationship—and some of our relationships with members of our families, both recent and in the past. We hoped that by analyzing how these relationships have grown and changed through the years, and sharing some of the lessons we've learned, others might be helped to sort their way through relationships that can be the richest—or the most painful—in their lives.

That day in the cafeteria with Mother, I decided that this just might be the most fun project I had ever participated in. In the words of Bo Pilgrim, King of Chickens and founder of Pilgrim's Pride, this could be "a mind-bogglin' thang."

Speaking the truth in love, we are to grow up
in all aspects into Him who is the head, even Christ.

—EPHESIANS 4:15 NASB

The Mother Voice

≈

"My mother influences my choices, even though she's not here to see what they are. I know what she thinks. I hear her voice when I clean my house, telling me where to put this and where to put that and not to sweep anything under the rug.

"I've always wanted to become a lawyer. But I hear my mother again, saying, 'How could you give up your job and abandon your family? How could you be away from me for two whole years?'

"No matter what I do, I always hear her voice. So I didn't clean my house so well—my rebellion. But I also didn't go to law school."

CHAPTER 1

Fowl Play

As long as I live, I shall never forget (my brother and sister will never forget, my now-husband-then-friend-at-church will never forget, quite possibly the entire city of Arlington, Texas, will never forget) the days my mother turned into a walking, talking, breathing, feathered chicken. Maybe I'm exaggerating, but only slightly so.

It was the early '70s, and other mothers had discovered "petal caps," nylon constructions designed to cover their hair on before-they-knew-what-to-call-them "Bad Hair Days." My mother, however, didn't purchase the petal-covered variety, which in our eyes would have been more than enough. Oh, no! She opted for one covered with white, farm-fresh chicken feathers. We told her it looked sick. She insisted she looked chic. We resorted to begging.

"Please, please, oh, heaven help us, PLEASE do not wear it in public," we begged. But she would have none of our squawking. Out the door she'd strut, feathered head held high with Pilgrim's Pride. There were moments back then when I felt certain my psyche would never, ever become unwarped. (There are those today who might say I had the diagnosis absolutely correct.) Certainly I vowed then I would not make the same sort of traumatizing mistakes with my own children. Little did I know that by the time kids become teenagers, parents can embarrass them by simply breathing.

For a few years I saw myself as doing quite well as a sensible mother. I recall a day when I went to pick up my sons Zach and Zeke after a visit with a little friend. They were around six and five, and they climbed into the front seat of the car with twin looks of disgust and disappointment. They evaluated their social interaction period as somewhat less than satisfactory. Zachary was the first to voice the most serious complaint.

"Mom, it was raining outside. There were GREAT mud puddles everywhere, and Jason's mother wouldn't EVEN let us go outside to play in them."

I mirrored their disgust, donning an expression of surprised horror. At that point, little Zeke joined his brother in a synchronized nod. Then he looked up at me, his brown eyes radiating awe and appreciation.

"I sure am glad you aren't sensible like all the other kids' moms."

I'm sure he thought he had handed me the compliment most likely to secure my place in the Mothers' Hall of Fame, and I guess I am pretty proud of it. After all, it's in my genes. When I was a grade-schooler, I felt I had a mother who was the envy of children far and wide. Well, at least from one end of our suburban cul-de-sac to the other. For starters, my mother was careful to teach us children an array of classical melodies, always sung in the voice of a wounded mezzo-soprano. One of my favorite arias went something like this:

> Oh, be kind to your web-footed friends,
> For a duck may be somebody's mother
> Who lives all alone in the swamp
> Where it's very cold and dahhhmp.
> Oh, you may think that this is the end.
> Well, it is.

As I write this, I'm moved to wonder what my mother's fascination with fowl indicated about her buried subconscious mind. At the time, however, I just enjoyed the fallout and shared the song with my best friend, a very blue-eyed, very blonde girl named Allison, who lived across the street. We sang it at the top of our lungs in ducklike, quacking voices as we walked arm in arm in a warm summer rain, splashing through puddles as we went.

Mother was also very careful to teach us the wisdom she had accumulated over the years of her eventful life, passing on a rich heritage of lore. I remember little Guides for Life such as, "Be alert." Why? "The world needs more Lerts." Goodbye kisses were always asked for in the following manner: "Kiss me, bucktooth—my tonsils itch." Now even my youngest son, Gabriel, asks me for kisses with the same line.

If we were very, very good children we were sometimes treated to another royal performance by my mother. She would first sit up very straight, adjusting her position to give us the best possible view. Then, gesturing gracefully, she would rub her index finger against her front teeth until they were completely and thoroughly dry. This had to be done with painstaking care or the stunt we were breathlessly awaiting would not work.

The grand finale came when she somehow managed to tuck her upper lip underneath itself so that it stuck in that attractive position, revealing her gums and front teeth. She then completed her entertaining exhibition by rapidly raising and lowering her eyebrows Charlie Chaplin–style, while sticking her tongue in and out of her mouth. She looked like some wild, animated rabbit. Could any child have wished for more?

As our teenage years approached, however, it was not always a many-splendored thing to have a mother who was somewhat left of center. I will refer to the feathered hat this one last time and then try to put it behind me. Eventually our mother hen finally came to her senses, and the poultry headdress ended up in the costume box. My siblings and I drew a collective sigh of relief, and in time, even this suffering in our young lives emerged as pure gold. With the addition of long underwear, a yellow, cone-shaped party hat for a beak, and a pair of yellow rubber gloves pulled over our toes for chicken feet, each of us kids won at least one first-place award at a variety of costumed affairs.

~

That was the early '70s. Fast-forward to the '90s, when I found myself playing the role of mom. There was the unforgettable day I forgot to wind up my wire headband and tuck it into a decorative knot as required. When I drove to the mall and went inside to pick up my kids, the two ends of the headband were sticking straight up in the air. As soon as the children spotted me, they grabbed me and hustled me into a dark hallway as quickly as possible (which reminded me of the way I acted the day I discovered one of my toddlers playing outside in the buff). There they explained to me indignantly that I, their mother, had shown up at the mall in our small town, where just about everybody knows us, looking for all the world like a large beetle with two polka-dot antennae sticking straight up in the air!

During that decade I also managed to humiliate my children simply by driving my car, which had 215,000 miles on its rusting body. As you can imagine, the appearance of the car itself would be embarrassing enough for them, but it also made obnoxious and humiliating noises. Let's see, how shall I put this in delicate terms?

Let's try this: Often when I run into the Get-It-Kwik to buy a soft drink or candy bar (and use my credit card for the purchase—doesn't everybody?), the clerk asks me a question that takes me slightly aback.

"Do you have gas too?"

"No," I respond, "that's just the way my car sounds. Sorry."

I once drove my children through Taco Bueno and gave our order to the invisible teen inside the loudspeaker box. "What was that?" the voice asked impatiently. Again I repeated our order. We continued our game of "Come again?" until finally, the exasperated voice said, "I'm sorry, ma'am, we can't hear you over the noise of your car. Would you mind turning off the engine?"

And when I drove up to the window to pick up our Mucho Burritos, I discovered I seemed to be alone in the car. Looking down, I saw all four of my children piled on the floorboard like a stack of pancakes, trying desperately not to be seen by their peers.

~

I now know it is inevitable that I will mortify my kids no matter what I do. I've come to grips with that. They'll be fine. After all, just look what a functional adult I turned out to be. For instance, when they whine about cleaning up their messes, I pull out my "cheery working songs" repertoire. I can do a lovely version of an English Mary Poppins trilling "A Spoonful of Sugar." I can also offer my personal favorite, sung in the voice of an overachieving dwarf, "Whistle While You Work." If my teenage sons happen to have guests, they respond by cranking their radios up full volume and working like wildfire to escape the house. A cruel trick, but effective.

When my daughter, Rachel, was in fourth grade, I visited her class to encourage them to take to writing, especially the writing of humorous stories. As a result, the class gifted me with a collective effort, a book titled *Lone Oak's Fourth Grade Funny Follies*. It was full of their funniest and most embarrassing moments. It's priceless. There's material enough for a couple of articles or maybe one good chapter. But I was most anxious to read what my own daughter had written. After all, there are so many stories from which to choose when you happen to be a member of our family. I was honored with a mother–daughter story. It follows here, exactly as Rachel wrote it.

> One afternoon in November, my mother and I were driving to Wal-Mart in the van. I saw two ladies talking in sign language. I thought it was neet and told my mother. She said "let's try it." I replied "Mother I havn't been too bad latly have I?" She laughed as she did all these strange signs. I ducked under the dash. "Your'e imbarrising me mom and yourself." I said. But she said in a greedy voice "I don't get imbarrissed." I moaned and ducked lower as she went on with her sign language. As you might already know I get imbarrised easily (Especailly with my mom.)
>
> —BY RACHEL FREEMAN, AGE 10

Ah, the warm memories my daughter's story brought to mind. The times I offered to pay Mother not to sing in the car. The ridiculous way she exercised in her pink negligee each evening, rolling on the floor from hip to hip with her hands held out to the side like an elegant ballerina. The unsensible way she let us play in the rain and splash in the mud. The way she'd tackle unsuspecting babies, toddlers, fourth-graders, and even teenagers, smothering them with hugs and kisses.

One Mother's Day I read an article in an old issue of *Reader's Digest* that struck a chord with me. It was titled, "My Mother Barked Like a Seal." Jeanmarie Coogan writes of her quintessentially embarrassing mom and ends the story by pointing to a childhood memory of her mother passing by a tree where a "bunch of us were dizzily swaying in the top branches." Rather than shrieking with fear, Jeanmarie's mother said, "I didn't know you could climb so high." Then she added, "That's terrific! Don't fall!" As the mother walked away, one boy, writes Jeanmarie, "spoke for us all. 'Wow,' he said softly. 'Wow.'"

Like Ms. Coogan, I also noticed as a child how my "friends, silent in their own homes, laughed and joked with my mother." And I was also blessed with a home where teenagers congregated, and their craziness simply added to the playful and ongoing banter.

Let's face it. Some of us were simply cursed with eccentric, erratic, embarrassing mothers. But, wow—didn't we have some fun?

God hath chosen the foolish things of the world
to confound the wise.

—1 CORINTHIANS 1:27 KJV

Mothers Are the Same
the World Over

~

PAUL REVERE'S MOTHER: "I don't care where you think you have to go, young man, midnight is past your curfew."

MONA LISA'S MOTHER: "After all that money your father and I spent on braces, that's the biggest smile you can give us?"

COLUMBUS'S MOTHER: "I don't care what you've discovered, you still could have written!"

MICHELANGELO'S MOTHER: "Can't you paint on walls like other children? Do you have any idea how hard it is to get that stuff off the ceiling?"

NAPOLEON'S MOTHER: "All right, if you aren't hiding your report card inside your jacket, take your hand out of there and show me."

ABRAHAM LINCOLN'S MOTHER: "Again with the stovepipe hat? Can't you just wear a baseball cap like the other kids?"

MARY'S MOTHER: "I'm not upset that your lamb followed you to school, but I would like to know how he got a better grade than you."

ALBERT EINSTEIN'S MOTHER: "But it's your senior picture. Can't you do something about your hair? Styling gel, mousse, something…?"

GEORGE WASHINGTON'S MOTHER: "The next time I catch you throwing money across the Potomac, you can kiss your allowance goodbye!"

JONAH'S MOTHER: "That's a nice story. Now tell me where you've *really* been for the last three days."

THOMAS EDISON'S MOTHER: "Of course I'm proud that you invented the electric lightbulb. Now turn it off and get to bed."

CHAPTER 2

Biker Babes

Have you seen the pictures in magazines of brother, sister, dad, and mom-with-baby-attached riding bicycles together as they tour Vermont-looking country roads? The caption often reads, "The Family that Plays Together Stays Together." I have always wondered what sort of caption would have gone under a picture of my family of origin just trying to mount and stay seated upon their bicycles. Probably "Tourist Accidents Waiting to Happen."

During the gasoline crisis of the mid-'70s, Mother became concerned that she was going to be stranded at home, planting tomato plants in her useless gas-guzzler. She persuaded Daddy to invest in a bicycle for each of them, failing to mention that she had never really learned to ride one.

On their first outing on the new bikes, Daddy took off through the neighborhood, assuming his wife was pedaling along behind him. He turned around just in time to see her nose-dive off the bike onto the grass. When he went back to check on her, she assured him she was unhurt and the fall had been a fluke.

"Not to worry," she said, remounting her bike and sticking her tongue out of the side of her mouth in deep concentration.

"Okay, here we go!" he said and rolled away. Feeling like a kid again, he was still looking forward to a ride in the evening breeze. "How you doin'?" he called back to Mother over his shoulder. There was, once again, silence. Feeling a little more anxious this time, he wheeled around to see her sitting on the sidewalk, her teased bun definitely askew and her kneecap bright pink. She looked, shall we say, daunted.

"Why didn't you tell me you didn't know how to ride a bicycle?" he yelled.

"Well, it looks so easy," she said, as if someone had been deliberately deceiving her.

"Look, Evel Knievel," Daddy said, "see if you can walk that thing back to the house without breaking your neck. There's more to riding a bike than meets the eye."

Then somewhere around the time of the arrival of my fourth baby, my sister, Rachel, went hunting and bagged a Big One—her husband, Scott St. John-Gilbert. We then learned what a sports fan really is. Up until this time, Daddy had been only mildly interested in watching football games on TV, and I had frequently observed all the Freeman males gather enthusiastically around the television for a major game only to find them all snoring in chorus by halftime.

Imagine our shock when gentlemanly Scott St. John-Gilbert joined our family and, during our first TV football game together, sent Mother almost through the ceiling with bellows that resembled those of a badly wounded water buffalo.

So now we have a sports fan on our hands who will arise at 6 A.M., run out on the porch in his skivvies—in sleet and snow—to bring in the sports page, check it out, and then return to bed for more sleep.

"Gilley," as I dubbed him since one Scott (my husband) in the family was confusing enough, was a fanatical San Francisco 49ers fan. He visited my parents one year in Texas when the 49ers were playing the Cowboys in Dallas, and of course going to the game was the opportunity of a lifetime. For some reason, his and my parents' seats were in the Cowboy stands, but Gilley was not about to be intimidated by the fact that he was totally surrounded by burly fans rooting for the opposite team. Mother told me later she was just thankful to get out alive.

~

As I have reviewed my family's sports history, I've been racking my brain trying to think of one sport involving physical movement that I have ever played with my mother. I vaguely remember spending a day with her at Girl Scout Camp, where we both tried our hands at archery. After twanging our wrists several times with the strings, almost poking each other's eyes out with the ends of the bows, and watching our arrows arc a full 12 inches each time we shot, we gave it up and retired to the shade of a tree and our favorite camping sport—whining about the heat, wondering when it would be time to roast marshmallows for our s'mores, and just generally wishing that the Powers That Be would let me have my Camping Badge so we could go home to do our nails. But there was more to come.

At trail-riding time, Mother's horse had her number long before she managed to mount him. You could almost see him yawn as he thought, *Oh, boy, another live one.* Once she was on board he promptly sat down and tried to roll over on her. I must say, I was impressed with her leap to safety. That did it, however. We threw in the towel, went home to blessed air-conditioning, gave ourselves manicures, and became Official Campfire Dropouts. There are other ways in life to get to eat s'mores.

Some years later, at a church camp when I was in junior high, I "had the opportunity" to try horseback riding again. Needless to say, childhood memories caused me to be somewhat nervous, fearing that my steed might also stop, drop, and roll.

I found myself wishing there were something more stationary than the horse to cling to, and I involuntarily grabbed an overhead branch as we were trotting along. The horse just kept right on going, and the branch, with me attached, slowly bent to the ground. I lay there in the dirt, flat on my back, still holding the branch to my chest and hollering, "Please don't step on me! Please don't step on me!"

When no thrashing hooves ground me into the turf, I finally got up the nerve to open my eyes. There, silhouetted against the blue sky, was my future brother-in-law, the Cowboy. He shook his head, said the cowboy equivalent of "tsk, tsk," and helped me up. And today, even though he (now old enough to sport an impressive handlebar moustache) has horses galore I could freely ride, I'm certainly thankful they don't depend on me for exercise.

By the time I had reached junior high, it was apparent I was never going to make any sports-type team. To begin with, I always—always—forgot at least part of my gym suit, and the punishment for this was that I didn't get to play anything, which, as you can imagine, almost broke my heart. During one open house, my PE coach cornered my mother for a conference.

"Mrs. Arnold, Becky has forgotten her gym suit for three weeks in a row now, and if she didn't have such a cute little way about her, I'd wring her neck."

"Why, thank you!" Mother responded, feeling that, in my case, a cute little way was going to be essential in getting me through life and that her at-home training in feminine charm had not gone to waste.

Even with my demonstrated lack of athletic ability, I usually got elected captain during basketball season because the Captain of the Team's duty was to make charts and decide whose day it was to play forward and whose day it was to play backward. Or something like that. Additionally, I've always been a diplomat of sorts, and I made everyone as happy as possible with their position on the team whatever it happened to be. Then I stood on the sidelines and cheered "my girls" on with bits and pieces of sporting advice I'd heard from television commercials.

"Go, team, go! Push 'em back, push 'em back, waaaaaay back. We need a goal! We need a ball! We need a touchdown! Whatever you can get! Rah, rah, rah!"

At the end of eighth grade, my long-suffering PE coach gave out awards to the girls: Most Athletic, Most Sportsmanlike, and so on. When I got my award, I wondered if it had ever been given before and if it might even have been created just for me. My award? Most Feminine.

Interestingly, Mother and Daddy both had a great time cheering for my athletically gifted younger siblings, Rachel and David, during their school baseball careers, and Mother either came to understand the game, or else she did a great imitation.

"Way to watch! Way to watch!" she'd yell in a most unfeminine manner. "Good save! Bring 'er in home now!" I'd have never guessed she had it in her.

Come to think of it, our family did have some success at playing whole-family games of croquet and occasionally even badminton—if we were not forced to break a sweat. Mother would also take us swimming and would actually get in the pool with us, but I never once, in all my life, saw her get a drop of water on her well-teased, French-twisted hair. It amazed me then and it amazes me now.

Her bicycle of the '70s finally went the way of the dehydrated food she kept stored in the attic, so at least I know my Tourist-Accident Mother is reasonably safe in her athletic pursuits these days. I gave up my own bike-riding career as well when, a couple of summers ago, I was attacked by a ferociously barking canine. Not knowing what to do, I frantically made a decision to try running over him with my front wheel. *That* was a mistake. I immediately found myself airborne—then face down on the pavement—and shortly thereafter, in a sling for two months with a broken arm.

So, Mom and I have raised the white flag on our handlebars and have chosen to pursue other, safer interests, like gardening and typing.

And this seems to be of some comfort to neighbors out for a walk who live within bike-riding distance of us.

Bodily exercise profits a little,
but godliness is profitable for all things.

—1 TIMOTHY 4:8 NKJV

"There's a woman inside me who wants to eat healthily and exercise regularly, but I can usually sedate her with chocolate."

—SOURCE UNKNOWN

CHAPTER 3

Sick Little Chicks

~

When I was a little girl, being sick (but not miserably so) was just about one of my favorite experiences. My mother turned into a Florence Nightingale. She read me stories and brought chopped ice for me to chew and bed trays so pretty that even dry toast and Jell-O looked like a gourmet treat. The highlight of each occasion was that the Honored Sick One was given the privilege of wearing Daddy's big, soft, yellow terry-cloth robe. It was almost enough to die for. (Certainly worth regurgitating for.)

If all of us kids happened to have the virus at the same time, we went into highly competitive theatrical performances, each one trying to out-writhe the other to secure the robe. As a matter of fact, when I saw the title of the bestselling novel *The Robe*, I was sure that it referred to the yellow terry-cloth garment hanging in my Daddy's closet. I've asked for no inheritance in my parents' estate save for this robe. It still hangs in my parents' hall closet, next to my wedding dress. When I spied it during my last visit to them, cozy, sentimental memories of nausea and fever tugged at my heart.

You can just imagine my shock, then, when I discovered that Scott's family did not celebrate headaches, colds, or viruses. As a matter of fact, when someone in Scott's family got sick they were expected to stay in bed and REST until they were well! No sneaking off to the mall for chicken soup at the cafeteria. No TV, board games, and undivided attention for a mere sniffle!

The first year we were married, Scott was at a complete loss over what to do with me when I came down with a fever and sore throat. He had never witnessed anything quite like the scene that opened up before him. He peeked into the bedroom where I lay moaning at appropriate intervals, my eyes closed, my open hand flung dramatically across my brow.

"Um...how ya doin' in here?" he asked nervously, wondering how on earth to handle a new bride with a head cold— one who, to all appearance, seemed to be on her deathbed.

In Shakespearean tones I replied, "Forgive me if I my small griefs magnify, but might I bother you for a small glass of water and an aspirin before I fade away into the deep, dark night?"

"Huh?" Scott asked.

"Come closer," I whispered, until he bent down next to my fevered brow. I continued, "Take me home to Mother. Then go far, far away."

He did so, and he continued to resort to this escape hatch for the first few years of our marriage. Then Mother moved away to Virginia, and we were stuck between a headache and a hard place. The inevitable happened, and I came down with an episode of the "vomitingmoblis." Amid loud clanging of pots and the wide-eyed stares of toddlers, Scott managed to prepare a bed tray for me. Never mind that it was a hamburger with a plateful of warm pork and beans mixed with mayonnaise and delivered on a cookie sheet—it was the thought that counted.

When I first came at Scott with a bed tray of cool washcloths, thermometers, medicine, bland-but-beautiful food, a magazine, flowers, and a mint, he looked at me as if I were an alien life-form. I eventually realized that his plea "Just leave me alone" psychologically translated to mean, "Just leave him alone."

~

As the years passed, we both tried harder to meet the needs of the other. On the one hand, I became a little more stoic and Scott gave nurturing his best shot. And I, on the other hand, came to accept that my husband truly preferred that I not fuss over him when he succumbed to illness.

So how have Scott and I come to handle the illnesses of our own children? Basically, our family is still somewhat schizophrenic in this area. It all hinges on whether we are discussing illness or accidents. At this writing, the kids and I are swimming down at the pier and I have just taken a scientific sampling on this matter. The question I posed from under my sunshades was direct and simple.

"Which parent do you want around when you are sick?"

Unanimously from under and above the lake water came the answer.

"You, Mom!"

Then I rephrased the question slightly. "Which parent do you want around when you've been hurt?"

The answer was just as forthright.

"Dad!"

Perhaps I should explain. When I hear a child screaming in pain as a result of injuring himself, my first reaction is to look around for any other adult or near-adult who can take over. I'm not proud of this, mind you, but I'm extremely queasy at the sight of blood.

If it turns out I must be the one to come to the aid of the victim, I always follow the same first-aid procedure. I arm myself with the biggest towel I can find, and then I walk backward toward the injured party in order to avoid even a glimpse of spurting blood. I toss the towel toward the victim like a bride throwing her bouquet and instruct the child to cover the wound. Once "it" is disguised, I am better able to render aid and comfort, one small step at a time. My motto is "What you can't see can't possibly hurt."

This method didn't work so well one time when Zach abruptly yelped in pain and came running into the kitchen holding one limp hand in the other. I immediately turned my back, grabbed a large kitchen towel, shut my eyes, and threw it over my shoulder in Zach's general direction. When I got up the nerve to peek, I saw that his hand was sufficiently intact, so I calmly walked over to him and applied pressure to his hand through the towel. He turned pale and screamed.

"Mom! Stop squeezing! It's not cut, it's broken!" A couple of X rays and $400 later, I discovered that his diagnosis was indeed correct. (So I'm not a paramedic!)

On another occasion, I had taken Zeke, Rachel Praise, and Gabriel with me to Cherry's, our local Christian bookstore. I led the troops toward the store, with Zeke bringing up the rear. As we were about to walk in the front door, I heard Zeke's voice behind me.

"Mom," he said, his voice sounding a bit worried, "I think I need to go to the hospital or something."

Because he was so calm, there was no verbal pre-warning to shut my eyes, and when I turned around, there Zeke stood with his leg split down his shin bone from kneecap to ankle, the skin rolled back like a scroll, exposing the bone. Fighting nausea, I hollered into the bookstore.

"My son just cut himself really bad on a license plate or something! Does anybody here have anything to put on it to help stop the bleeding?"

I then ran to the van and grabbed whatever makeshift dressing for Zeke's wound I could find from the backseat, surprising myself by my clear head. At the same time, three ladies came out the store, each carrying what they could contribute to the cause, with one woman even praying over Zeke by the time I reached him. When I finally got my son in to the doctor for stitches, the nurses were in stitches themselves.

"Did you know," asked the head nurse, "that I pulled a roll of paper towels, a disposable diaper, a box of Kleenex, a T-shirt, a dish towel, and several grass clippings off your son's leg? What were you trying to do—suffocate the wound?"

Remember, I have never advertised that I am a Rock in a Crisis. But I can generally be counted on to supply entertainment for the wounded. Along with a nice bed tray and a big, soft, terry-cloth robe.

A merry heart doeth good like a medicine.

—Proverbs 17:22 KJV

Mom Runs the Best
Hospital in the World

~

All of us moms and daughters will have to care for someone who is ill or infirm at some time. Beloved author Edith Schaeffer raises this sort of nurturing to an art, with plenty of understanding of our limitations as caretakers as well. ("Comfort yourself by saying, 'I am limited, I am finite, I can only do one thing at a time...'" she writes.)

I could not recommend a book more highly than the classic *What is a Family?* It is still in print after 25 years. For gentle ideas in caring for a 2-year-old with a cold or an 82-year-old with a broken hip, the chapter "A Shelter in the Time of Storm" is timeless and inspiring. Here's a little sample:

> For some people the memory of illness carries with it the memory of loving care, cool hands stroking the forehead, sponge baths in bed, clean sheets under a hot chin, lovely-flavored drinks, alcohol backrubs...Flowers near the bed, curtains drawn when fever is hurting the eyes, soft singing of a mother's or father's voice during a sleepless night...There are some amazingly sharp descriptions given as to what will be counted as things which have been done directly for Him. Among them are: I was thirsty, and ye gave me drink...I was sick, and ye visited me.

CHAPTER 4

We Rose and Called Her Blessed

~

Hi!" I cheerfully greeted my mother on one of our lunch days, but I couldn't help noticing she looked a bit haggard. "How was your visit with Grandmother and Grandaddy Arnold this weekend?"

"Grandad was great, as usual. As far as the visit with your Grandmother Arnold goes, I feel like I've been entertaining a junior-high prima donna. Very strange phenomenon," she finished, shaking her head. "Let's just find a nice, quiet table and order something without having a scene with the waitress, okay?"

I laughed, knowing that most trips out to eat with Grandmother Arnold—Mom's mother-in-law—usually involved some tension with the unfortunate waiter or waitress on duty that day. He or she could not know that all efforts to please would be futile.

When my mother took a mother-in-law at the tender age of 19, she had a less than realistic view of older women. For one thing, Mom's mother (my "Nonnie") was by then 62 years of age, and Nonnie was at her best and most mature self, approaching sainthood. Mother had assumed that all women everywhere mysteriously entered into sainthood somewhere around middle age. She had great difficulty understanding that her husband's mother, my Grandmother Arnold, was a chubby elfin of a woman who had, basically, never grown up.

Mother spent the first 20 years of her marriage periodically fussing with my Grandmother Arnold, and periodically enjoying her. She had a cute personality, she loved to go places and do things, and she liked to play table games as much as Mother did. But she had a strange self-centeredness and an uncanny ability to say the wrong thing at the wrong time.

I'll have to admit that, even as a child, I had to notice—my Grandmother was a *case*, by almost any standard. Even when I was alone with her as a little girl, I always had the oddest sense that I was the more adult of the two of us. Now, that wasn't always a bad thing to me. Actually, it was often kind of fun.

To me, Grandmother Arnold was jolly and huggable and much too short to be intimidating, even to the smallest child. She was like a round, fluffy Chatty Cathy doll. Only there was no "Off" button at the back of her neck, and her batteries never ran out. But I was free to run out to play when I tired of her endless chatter.

Mother, unfortunately, was not. On many of Grandmother's visits, I'm sure there were times when Mother would have gladly run out the door and joined me in climbing the nearest tree—in spite of her lack of athletic agility. Alas, many women must come to accept that their mother or mother-in-law is incapable of being what they need—or want—her to be. Thankfully, there is usually someone, some motherly figure, who can fill in the gaps somewhat—if we are open to God meeting this need outside of our family tree.

For my mother, Nonnie was nurturing and wise enough to make up for the shortcomings of her mother-in-law. Thinking of this, I smiled, patted my mom's hand, and said, "Sounds like you need a trip to see Nonnie."

Mother grinned. "Maybe so. Nonnie is so soothingly…traditional," she sighed. "She's my generation's idea of what a mother and grandmother ought to be. She even looks the part—plump, that beautiful silver hair worn in a bun, print housedress—even the apron to go with it!

"She's always been there when I, or most anybody else, needed her. As kids, we were always able to take Nonnie totally for granted in a wonderfully comforting way. We had very little of this world's goods, but we did have her. We knew she'd be at home when we left for school and almost always at home when we came back at the end of the day. On the rare occasions when we came home and she wasn't there, the day seemed cold and uneasy until she got back."

Mother was plainly in the mood to talk that day, and even though the clock was ticking toward pick-up time at my kid's school, I wanted to join in her memories and learn things I'd never known before about my grandmother.

Mother sipped her fresh coffee and then grinned. "Thinking of the past few days, I think Nonnie's greatest gift has been knowing how to listen!"

"Yep," I empathized, "you need a trip to Sweetwater and a big-bosomed hug from Nonnie."

"Soon," she nodded. "Seriously, though, people found this gift of rapt attention to be a healing gift in itself. She simply listened, made little sympathetic noises, and poured coffee and served cake or pie, and they went away comforted. Her major source of profound advice was a slow, 'Well, things have a way of workin' out for the best.'

"When I was in junior high, my brother Joe fell off a rooftop where he was working and suffered a head injury. Over a period of months, his health deteriorated. He died in what was called, at the time, an iron lung—in a charity hospital in Dallas. Nonnie went about doing what had to be done, and I only occasionally saw quiet tears spill from those beautiful blue eyes.

I never saw her break down, but whenever she talked about him over the years, her eyes brimmed with tears.

"One of the things I learned from her then was that all things in life can be borne. She brought Philippians 4:13 alive for me: 'I can do all things through Christ which strengtheneth me.' Those qualities of hers are part of my inheritance—from a mother who was rich in many ways other than cash." Mother smiled and paused, remembering.

How interesting, I thought. So my mother still heard her mother whispering over her shoulder, too—on this occasion, whispers of courage in a crisis.

My own heart warm with remembering, I flashed back to a time when I was a teenager at a family reunion at Nonnie's house. The scene unfolded for me as if it were in the present.

Mother and Daddy, and all my aunts, uncles, and cousins, are scattered around the living room sitting on couches, lounging on the carpet, or leaning against the walls. The setting sun casts a rosy glow that comes to rest gently on Nonnie's face. She rocks contentedly in her comfy chair, surrounded by her children and grandchildren. Softly, a male voice, the deep baritone of one of my uncles, begins to sing.

"When peace like a river attendeth my way…" Raised in a church where the singing was a cappella, Nonnie and her grown children fill the room with rich harmony.

"When sorrows like sea billows roll…" The beautiful texture of the well-loved hymn saturates the room with a holy presence. "Whatever my lot, Thou hast taught me to say, it is well, it is well, with my soul." Times of serenity, times of suffering. It is well, it is well. Because one day, "our faith shall be sight." On that day—the hymnist's words, full of come-what-may confidence, declare—"the trump shall resound and the Lord shall descend. Even so, it is well with my soul."

I knew then that, no matter what the future might hold, the roots in our Family Tree would hold. Nonnie had tilled the soil well for faith to grow and had left future generations of females with a legacy of love and hope that would go on and on—even through disappointment and grief beyond comprehension. For it is true, ultimately—things do have a way of workin' out for the best.

And we know that in all things
God works for the good of those who love him,
who have been called according to his purpose.

—ROMANS 8:28

Daughters Remember

~

Our mother gave us the absolute assurance
that we were loved, that life at its darkest
has moments of laughter and light,
that nothing happens in life
that cannot be borne with Christ's help.

—RUTHIE ARNOLD, BECKY'S MOM

I asked Aunt Etta (my mom's big sister) to write a fun memory
of Nonnie—and was delighted to receive the following anecdote.

Nonnie and I lived through the Great Depression surrounded by men—my father and five brothers. I was the only
girl until my little sister, Ruthie, was born, the year I turned 13.
It was expected that the oldest daughter would don an apron
and help Nonnie in the kitchen, so of course I did. A meal for
eight always presented a major problem, since everyone in our
small town was poor and my father adamantly refused to "go
on relief."

I watched my mother make a breakfast for eight out of
cornmeal poured into boiling water. Mush. Mush was good
with syrup—if you had any. If not, you stirred sugar into it,
and if you were lucky enough to have spices, cinnamon. I
watched her save any leftover mush to fry for the evening meal.
I never saw her throw one biscuit away. "They'll be good split
and toasted in the oven tonight," she reminded me.

Many years later, married, I returned to Sweetwater for
Thanksgiving. As always, I arrived the night before to help prepare the turkey, cook cornbread for the dressing, and so on.

Nonnie and I enjoyed a warm mother–oldest daughter time planning for the next day's avalanche of my siblings—their children—and my children.

The Thanksgiving dinner was perfect—a huge turkey, brown and succulent. Dressing that melted in your mouth. Cranberry sauce, fruit salad, and desserts so rich they were almost immoral. I thought of those spartan days during the Depression and thanked the good Lord that our mother no longer was forced to scrimp, to make water gravy and mush.

While carrying dishes to the kitchen, I noticed a spot on the floor. Bending over, I examined it closely. Dressing? Someone had dropped it, and someone else had stepped in it. Disgusting! "What on earth is this?" I asked.

Nonnie, who was close behind me, leaned over my shoulder. "Whatever it is, save it."

I collapsed with laughter. The others filed in one by one—my family cannot bear to hear chuckling and chortling and not know the reason. When I told them, the house rang with laughter.

To this day, we share this story with new members of the family, and it will be passed on and on and on and...

CHAPTER 5

Off to a Sizzlin' Start!

News travels fast in our small town, and when word got out that I had coauthored a book about worms—*Worms in My Tea*—my status immediately grew. As a matter of fact I found myself proudly introduced in public places as "the author with *Worms*." Another friend came up with a promotion ploy—suggesting Mother and I wear buttons that read "Ask us about our Worms."

With that sort of interest, of course, invitations to speak began to pour in. Well, perhaps *trickle* might be a more accurate word for it. (Okay, so I dropped a hint over the phone to the Ladies' Committee Chairwoman from my church that I just might be available to speak at our annual Ladies' Class Christmas Coffee.)

When I arrived at the home where the coffee was to take place, it looked like it belonged to Martha Stewart on one of her better Christmases. Elegant it was, with a roaring fire in the huge stone fireplace, luxurious furniture covered in rich tapestries, and the entire house accented with holly, ivy, lace, candles, flowers—the works.

By a great miracle I had arrived early, and I soon saw that the hostesses were having trouble with the spout of the gorgeous silver coffee urn. It would not stop dripping. There it stood in the middle of the white damask cloth, nicely lit by a votive candle on either side, its spout creating a puddle in a hastily placed crystal punch cup. I couldn't help thinking that perhaps the Spirit had prompted me to arrive early because He had foreseen my skills would be needed. (Readers of *Worms in My Tea* will already know that I have become somewhat of an expert on leaking things—appliances, car radiators, commodes, sewers. Why wouldn't these skills transfer to an elegant silver coffee urn?)

I jiggled the spout in a more professional manner than the hostess had been jiggling it, and when the puddle continued t) grow, I bent low and tried to peer up the spout itself. Clearly I was onto something. A most peculiar odor became apparent—it was followed by a puff of smoke wafting before my eyes. Suddenly the hostesses sprang at me from all directions, beating me about the head and shoulders with towels and tossing cups of water in my general direction. When I realized I had managed to ignite my own hair with the votive candles beside the urn, I did exactly what I had taught my first-graders to do in our "Safety First" course: I stopped, dropped, and rolled all the way to an easy chair where the hostesses insisted I stay until it was time for me to speak.

"We don't want anything else to happen, Becky," they assured me. I was touched by their concern.

My topic for the morning was, "Taking Time to Wonder As You Wander Through the Season," and I'm sure the ladies were indeed wondering why the hostess had included fragrance of singed hair in the potpourri on her tables. (Considering the elegance of the rest of her decorations, I expect we may have seen the evolution of an entirely new Christmas fragrance. I watch for it every year. It transports one almost immediately to a stable.)

I had planned to end my talk with a moving quote about the love of a father for his young son. At this tender, emotion-charged moment, the Sterno heater on the buffet table suddenly ignited, shooting flames about two feet into the air. It created quite a stir, but our Christmas Coffee Women's Volunteer Fire Department leaped into action, beating the flames with dish towels, trying to subdue the inferno with crystal cups full of punch and coffee, and finally extinguishing the persistent flames with an inverted fondue pot.

When the hostesses looked in my direction, I was thankful I had been standing at least three yards from the table during the entire event.

Afterward I went straight home, called my mother, gave her all the details of my first speech, and told her how we might need to bring portable fire extinguishers to any future events we might do together. She laughed, I laughed, and then in the background, I could hear my father asking for details. "So, how'd Becky do?"

Though her voice was a bit muffled, I could heard her praise me as only a truly creative mother can: "Honey, she was on fire. The audience simply melted in her hair…uh…I mean *hands*."

He…makes…His ministers a flame of fire.

—HEBREWS 1:7 NKJV

CHAPTER 6

Lucy & Ethel
Speak Up

~

In the spring following the Christmas buffet, Mother and I were invited to speak at a mother–daughter banquet at a church in the pretty little East Texas town of Kilgore. Daddy decided to drive us there, rather than risk having the Kilgore police eventually called out to look for the Two Lost Speakers. I sat in the backseat enjoying the peace and quiet and wondering how Scott was faring back at the ranch with our four kiddos. Mother, however, had her mind on the speaking engagement.

"Don't you think we should do a little coordinating of what we might say? I have my speech all typed out," she informed me with satisfaction. "It's right here in this folder." She was holding onto it tightly.

"You wrote out every word?" I asked.

"Oh, yes," she replied like a seasoned pro. "I don't plan to read it, but I just feel more comfortable if I have the entire speech before me in black and white. The audience will hardly notice. Since you'll be speaking first, I'll just put it on the speaker's stand before the banquet starts, and it will be there when my turn comes." It seemed to me she was doing it the hard way, but I decided not to tell her so. I'm independent, but I'm not foolhardy.

When we arrived, Mother pointed out that I had managed to get ballpoint pen ink on my white blouse, dead center. I was also wearing a vest which I had left unbuttoned because it was too tight.

"Becky," Mother decided, "if you don't mind having your chest crushed I think we can button the vest over the stain. It will be good practice for when you get your first mammogram. What do you think?" From the look in my eyes, she must have decided she didn't really want to know what I thought, and she went on. "Maybe you could make your speech while taking very shallow breaths?"

We decided to go with this idea, and I glanced with something akin to envy at Mother's flowingly comfortable and spotless hot-pink knit dress with the lavender bow at the waist—and was absolutely delighted to discover a moist, half-consumed breath mint nestling in the bow, just about even with her belly button.

"Mother!" I hissed, "You've got to stop drooling and learn to hang on to your breath mint if you want to make any kind of impression at this nice banquet!" She was unperturbed. Raising the one eyebrow she raises so well, she gave me a nonchalant smile, peeled the mint off her lavender belt, and popped it back into her mouth.

As soon as we arrived at the church, Mother hurried up front to check out the speaker's stand and to place her folder of notes just so.

I spoke first. Because I had several books from which I read a number of touching quotes and excerpts, when I brought my speech to a close I had a little difficulty getting everything together. I had a large stack of cattywampus papers, books, and visual aids to take with me back to my seat. I soon began to feel as though I were packing for a trip through the Yukon in front of an audience that seemed to be growing restless. Before it was all together, I got my wrist tangled in an electric cord and dropped one book (a hardback) on my foot, but I left the podium as clean as a whistle.

Mother stepped to the podium, cleared her throat, and turned panic-stricken eyes in my direction. "Ahem," she said. "Becky, dear, do you have my notes?"

Feeling like Lucy Ricardo responding to Ethel in some crazy sitcom, I sheepishly produced the cherished papers and delivered them to Mother at the podium. I promise I didn't take them with me on purpose! By that point in the afternoon, I'm sure Mother would have gladly rented me a private nest in someone else's family tree.

Afterward, the ladies and their daughters were polite and kind, but no one gushed. (It should be noted that Mother and I require copious gushing.) However, Daddy came through for us, doing the best job of gushing a man can do. During the two-hour drive back home, he stopped at a handy country cafe to treat us to a relaxing dinner.

Since the cafe was about the only one in this neck of the woods, and since it was Saturday night, a stream of harried waitresses carrying plate after plate of chicken-fried steak and cream gravy kept bursting through the swinging doors from the kitchen. Forty-five minutes later, none of those plates had been ours, so I asked Mother if she had any of her breath mints left I could munch on.

"Preferably one from your purse rather than your belly button," I specified. After eating a few mints I excused myself to go to the ladies' room, which seemed to be occupied. At least, when I tugged on the door it didn't open, so I leaned against the wall and waited. Soon a cute little cowgirl, about 18, joined me in my vigil. I said "Hi," but she didn't seem to want to chat, so we lapsed into silence. And lapsed. And lapsed. Finally, an idea occurred to me.

"Wouldn't it be funny if no one was in there? You and me standing out here, twiddling our thumbs, waitin' all this time? Wouldn't that be funny?" With that, the cowgirl reached out, took firm hold of the doorknob, gave it a twist and— Shazam!—the door flew open. She turned hard eyes upon me.

"How 'bout that?" I giggled. "Not a soul was in there after all."

With an expression of contempt she stomped into the restroom, closing the door in my face. I distinctly heard her say, "You goon!" And I had been in line first!

Well, I did what any self-assured, assertive woman of the '90s would do. I went back to my parents' table and told my Daddy on her. Daddy said I most certainly was not a goon and would have gone to defend my honor had I not held him back. I felt a little better, but I couldn't help wondering if a brief history of my speaking career might be summed up in one simple sentence: Hair today, goon tomorrow.

Wherefore, my beloved brethren,
let every man be swift to hear, slow to speak...
—JAMES 1:19 KJV

Chapter 7

My Father,
the Saint

As a young bride, I wrote a letter to our local newspaper to nominate my daddy, George Arnold, as "Father of the Year." Among other things, I wrote, "Daddy is the tenderest, most loving man I know…He never leaves for work without kissing our mother goodbye, and he greets her with a warm embrace when he comes home. Every day of my life he told me he loved me and that all of us children were precious to him…My father is also the wisest man I know…He has a living, vital relationship with the Lord and has encouraged each of us in our Christian walk. Daddy has a wonderful sense of humor…" and so on. Quite a tribute, but how would you have liked to have been the new son-in-law?

Now Scott loves my father (it can't be helped!) but it drove him nuts trying to measure up to the standard of the father-in-law he sometimes lovingly refers to as "St. George." How could anyone compete with this gentle Big Bird of the Arnold Family Nest?

A number of years back, when our family was on vacation at Holly Lake in our beloved East Texas, I was sitting on the deck of our rented condo with my husband, Scott; my brother,

David, and his wife, Barb; and my sister, Rachel, and her husband, Gilley.

We could see Daddy down on the dock with his grandkids and knew he would be patiently putting worms on hooks for Gabriel, our then seven-year-old budding fisherman. He would also have plenty of lines to untangle for Rachel Praise, our only female child, a half-hearted fisherwoman at best. If our preteen sons, Zach and Zeke, had a problem it would probably be the hardest of all to solve—retrieving expensive lures from the branches of tall trees. All of these chores Daddy would have to manage while trying to make sure David's and Barb's little Tyler didn't fall in the water. Naturally enough, our conversation on the deck turned to St. George the Divine.

My memory drifted back to the time when our family had just discovered this pine-covered paradise at Holly Lake, and if I squinted just right in the evening sun, Daddy's silver-streaked hair looked almost 1969-black again. The voices of my own children faded to the long-ago sounds of David, Rachel, and me teasing and fussing and vying for Daddy's attention. As I watched the fuzzy evening scene, with my thoughts drifting from Now to Then and back again, I was suddenly pulled from my reverie by David's deep chuckle.

"Hey, Rachel, remember that time you thought you had a huge bass and pulled your pole so hard you brought up about a gallon of seaweed? It hit Dad right upside the head! He turned real slow toward us, deadpan, with his head covered with green gook. Man, I thought I'd lose it!"

"Yeah, well," Rachel spoke up, having decided quickly that the best defense would be a good offense, "don't forget the night Dad took you fishing 50 miles out in the country. As I recall, you topped off a long day in the hot sun by dropping the car keys in the lake." David grinned, bit off a piece of fishing line, and went back to tying a lure, but Barb definitely wanted to pursue that topic.

"What did George say when David did that?" she asked.

"Oh," Rachel laughed, "I think he said something like, 'Aw…son, I can't believe you did that. I just told you to be careful when I handed them to you! Remember?' And that was the extent of the bawling out. Dad telephoned Mom from a marina, and she somehow managed to find us in the dark and bring an extra set of keys. By the time she got there, Dad was laughing about it and even had David tickled. He's got the patience of a—"

"Saint?" Scott asked, throwing a "see what I'm up against" look in my direction.

"Yeah," I laughed, determined to give Scott a more balanced view of my Dad. "Sure, he's unique. But nobody's perfect!"

The faces staring back at me looked unconvinced.

"Well, okay, let's think. He must have a fault…I know! He hated working on cars. I once heard him say 'darn' when the hood slammed down on his head."

"Good try," Rachel said, "but even though he hated it, when David and I both got our driver's licenses, he spent most of his Saturdays keeping three used cars running."

"Touché," I admitted. "File that under 'Self-Sacrificing: Looking Out for the Needs of Others.'"

"Okay, guys," interrupted Rachel's husband, Gilley, "he's gotta have some faults."

Scott reached over to pat the greenhorn son-in-law on the back. "Listen, Gilley, I've been at this son-in-law business a few years now and I'll just save you some time here by asking a few questions: Have you ever seen George mad? Grouchy? Worried? In a hurry?"

Gilley thought over each question, then shook his head in amazement. "Come to think of it, I've never even seen him in an outfit that wasn't completely color-coordinated."

I scratched my head. "He must have some sort of flaw. I know he does…"

"Bound to," David agreed.

"Let me think a minute..." said Rachel.

Just then Mother came out of the house to join us, iced tea in hand. "Okay, Mom," Rachel challenged, "tell us some of Dad's worst faults! Don't hold anything back. We're all adults now. No use shielding us from the truth. We can take it, whatever it is."

Mother frowned, turned her chaise lounge away from the sun, pulled up a table for her tea, and stretched out. We could see she was thinking hard, and the silence hung heavy as we waited with great expectation for our father's deepest darkest secrets to be revealed. Just as I was about to nod off, she spoke hesitantly.

"Well...he is a slow eater."

I feigned a heartbreaking sob. "Oh, Mother! You've absolutely ruined our image of Daddy. How could we ever love him now, after such a horrifying confession!"

"I guess that's not too hard to live with," she conceded. "I've gotten a lot of mending done over the years waiting for him to finish his meals."

"What's 'mending'?" Scott asked before I could slap my hand across his mouth. Suddenly it was I who was in the "let's compare" hot seat. This same sort of question had come up before, over another activity that Mother continued to insist on performing—"dusting," I believe, was the antiquated term she used. But I was ready this time with a life-saving definition for "mending."

"Scott, honey," I said with perfect equanimity, "mending was a quaint old-fashioned form of entertainment for pre-modern woman. Before the invention of television. And the wheel." Then I quickly steered the conversation back to Mother. "Think hard, woman!"

"There is one other thing that comes to mind," she said thoughtfully. "He never can find anything, even when I tell him exactly where it is. For years, no matter what he was looking for, he would go to the cabinet I described, open it, and stand there gazing into it."

"No!" we all gasped simultaneously.

"Yes!" Mother was hot on the trail now, thinking she'd uncovered a really dastardly habit. "'It's not here!' he would say. He would always say, 'It's not here!' and then I would have to stop what I was doing and go stand beside him, reach into the cabinet, and hand him the item. Then he would say, 'Oh.'"

"How did you ever cope?" Rachel exclaimed in exaggerated shock. "Did you think of divorce?"

"I finally taught him to say 'I don't see it' instead of 'It's not here!' and our relationship was saved." By this time, Mother was visibly worn with the trauma of reliving her nightmare. Barb was not impressed.

"Is that it?" she asked. "That's his one fault?"

Mom wiped the perspiration off her forehead. She was really racking her brain now. "Well, I guess by today's standards I have spoiled him pretty badly. I do cut his hair, lay out his clothes every morning, fix his cereal." *Oh, mother—please*, I thought. *Impressionable young husbands are listening to this.* "Why, I even lay out his vitamins and fill a glass with water and leave it with them on the counter. I really fouled him up not long ago, though. I forgot to put his water glass out. He came into the kitchen, looked at his vitamins, then looked at me in genuine puzzlement as if he didn't quite know what to do.

"'Where's my water?' he asked. I couldn't believe it!

"'I keep it in the faucet!' I said, my voice dripping sarcasm."

That's tellin' him, Mother, I thought. *Mark up one point for the independent little woman!*

"Well," said Barb, "what did George say to that?"

Mother looked sheepish for a minute, then answered quietly, "I sort of forgot what he said after he laughed and laughed and then grabbed me around the waist and kissed me and told me how funny I was."

Basically, our discussion boiled down to this: I'm okay, you're okay, Mother's okay, and Daddy's—almost perfect.

But evidently all three of his children had momentarily blanked out what it was like to take a cross-country automobile tour with St. George.

Each one should test his own actions.
Then he can take pride in himself,
without comparing himself to somebody else.
—Galatians 6:4

CHAPTER 8

Head 'Em Up,
Move 'Em Out,
Tie Him Up

∾

Recently my friend—let's just call her "Please Don't Use My Name, My Mother Would Have a Fit"—called and asked me to please shoot her in the foot if it ever crossed her mind to take a vacation with her parents again. "How I have managed to tie my own shoes, the strings unbleached and unstarched as they are, my mother will never know…"

Please Don't Use My Name's call threw me into a spell of reverie, recalling a trip that I, an adult of fairly sound mind, took with my own fairly functional parents. Harking back to the conversation with my brother and sister regarding my father's perfection, the three of us, as I said, had evidently forgotten what it was like to take a cross-country automobile tour with St. George.

On the particular trip I am remembering, I was no longer a child. In fact, I had three of my own by then—Zach and Zeke, aged four and three, and Rachel Praise, my teething baby daughter. All three were, unfortunately, complete foreigners to the concept of "sit still." Scott, to his everlasting gratitude, was unable to join us for the voyage east.

By the time we would reach our destination—my parent's home in Virginia, some 1500 miles from Texas—Mother, Daddy, and I would all be suffering from various degrees of dementia. I, in a delirious moment at a mealtime break, prayed fervently that the prizes in my sons' Kiddie Burger Boxes might be duct tape and child-sized straitjackets.

At least one of the things I had forgotten about my father was that this easygoing, laid-back, *Happy Days* man would undergo an amazing transformation when we went on vacation.

St. George the Divine would suddenly become Tough Trail Boss of the Covered (Station) Wagon, trying to get the herd to Montana before winter snows set in. When the need for a treat or a comfort station became acute, we kids knew to watch for a gas station or cafe on the "right" side of the freeway. It was as if Daddy had never learned to turn around or use freeway crossover bridges. Over the years, as we would dig once again into the stale-cracker-and-peanut-butter rations from the backseat, I would wonder if it was my father who had coined the term "Meals on Wheels."

When this memory of my father, long submerged in the dark recesses of my childhood mind, sprang forth while I was preparing for this more recent trip, I began to plan ahead. With stopwatch in hand, I took to positioning the kids with their noses pressed to the right-hand windows, training them to yell "I see one, Grandpa George!" with split-second timing. But we were no match for Daddy's quick-draw excuses.

"Sorry, Little Hombres," Daddy would apologize faster than a speeding silver bullet. "Can't get there from here!"

"But Daddy!" I wailed after watching gas station after gas station, café after café, whiz by with hardly a split second's hesitation. Eventually, I was forced to accept the Law of the New Concrete Frontier: Every gas station and cafe in America is built on the wrong side of the highway.

So you can understand my deep sense of gratitude and relief when we circled the wagon and stopped for a rest at a shopping center in Staunton, Virginia. We came close to experiencing our first stampede as we elbowed each other out of the way to get inside to wide-open, air-conditioned SPACE! There we bought lunch, treats, and diapers, and just generally let the kids loose on the unsuspecting mall.

Once Cowboy Daddy had rounded us back into the wagon amid shouts of "Head 'em up, move 'em out!" Mother and I each tried to persuade him to let one of us drive for a while. If only he would have allowed one of us to escape the back recesses of the station wagon where babies cried and pooped and whined and wrestled, it would have been a respite and a privilege. When Daddy refused to let go of the reins, Mother and I discussed forming a two-woman posse to calf-rope and hog-tie him. We'd make him think *Rawhide...*

But, to his great credit, my father had kept his good humor on the trip, and in every other possible way had done what he could to keep the peace. It was as if he somehow sensed the warm winds still a-blowin' and knew the snows would come later this year in Montana. He'd drive the hands steadily on—ignoring the intermittent bellowing of the females and young in his charge—at a pace that would reach the homeplace safe and sound and in good time.

Once we had hit the unlonesome trail again—wonder of wonders, miracle of miracles—all three kids dropped off to sleep simultaneously! I took the opportunity to scrunch down in the backseat, propping up my bare feet between the heads of Mother and Daddy sitting up front as I prepared to join my Wynken, Blynken, and Nod in Slumberland.

Contemplating my parents in the evening light, I finally relaxed. But sleep didn't come as quickly as I had anticipated, and so I rested by closing one eye and squinting at my father through the opening between my left big toe and the one next to it. I tried to imagine him as mother had once described him in his heyday—a "Fonzie" of the '50s. Now, with the passage of time, he looked remarkably like former Texas Senator Phil Gramm.

Through the opening between the toes on my right foot, the once brown-haired teenybopper from Sweetwater High's Class of '55 now resembled another of Texas's senators—silver-haired Kay Bailey Hutchison.

Just as I was about to doze off, Rachel Praise stirred—and I could detect a telltale odor rising. I looked on the floor of the car for the new sack of diapers I had bought at the shopping center. They were not there. Fighting panic, I began to paw around under mounds of toys, pillows, suitcases, and blankets. It was no use.

"Whoa, Daddy! Stop the car!" I yelped. "I think I left the diapers on the top of the car when we were at the mall!"

Daddy reluctantly slowed the station wagon at the next turnaround (aha—he did know how to do it!). Sure enough, the diapers had apparently ridden shotgun on top of the wagon for a couple of miles out of Staunton before blowing off and landing on the side of the road. Can't you just hear the conversation in the car behind us?

"Oh, land's sake, Henry, duck! We're about to be flattened by Industrial-Size Huggies!"

"Ya don't reckon they're loaded, do ya, Ethel?"

CHAPTER 9

We're Out of Our Minds—Be Back in Five Minutes

~

To my enormous relief, we spotted the diapers by the side of the road only 20 miles back. I was delighted to see the diapers, but not delighted that we were going to have to redo those miles with the pleasure of now wide-awake company. Daddy managed to stay John Wayne–cool, while Mother did what mothers do to make everybody feel better. She began a "did I ever tell you about the time…" story guaranteed to make me appear to have the intelligence of a neurosurgeon compared to her at my age.

"If you think," she began, "that allowing your father to drive down the highway with a bag of diapers the size of a small glacier on top of his car is forgetful and embarrassing, wait 'til I tell you about the time your daddy and I took our first trip with Grandmother and Grandaddy Arnold. Right after we were married, we drove with them from Sweetwater to the Gulf Coast to visit relatives—the kind of 'luxury vacation' most people took back in those days.

"It was late May, and already too hot for comfort. I soon learned that my new little mother-in-law had absolute, unquestioned control over the air-conditioning. At what seemed like three-minute intervals, she would announce 'IT'S HOT!' and with a flick of her tiny hand, the car would become a freezer on wheels.

"At the time I didn't know about menopausal ladies and couldn't figure out why she would declare it was HOT and, three seconds later, decide it was cold. I was used to a mother who hardly ever expressed a want or desire of her own and who almost always deferred to the comfort of others. I somehow felt that the rest of us were entitled to some opinion on the temperature once in a while, but Grandad never said a word.

"I thought indignantly, *It might help if you would say something like, 'It seems warm to me. Is anybody else, perhaps, a bit warm too?'* This was the first of many silent dialogues I had with my mother-in-law.

"She also expected frequent potty stops and pie-and-coffee stops just about every hour on the hour, which I thought was a good idea—but stopping so often was a little hard on your grandad. They didn't call him 'Speedy' for nothin'. It suited me fine. Gave me a chance to thaw out.

"We were facing a nine-hour drive, and after five hours or so, Grandaddy Arnold let your daddy drive. When he pulled to the side of the road to change drivers, I got out of the backseat, intending to sit beside your daddy in the front. My new father-in-law frowned.

"'Ruth Ann,' he said with a warning in his voice, 'George needs to keep his mind on his driving.'

"'I promise I won't bother him,' I said, and scampered into the front seat beside my new husband. And I thought I did rather well for several miles. But we were 19 and newly wed, and had a lot to talk about, and most of it was funny so there was perhaps a bit more giggling than appropriate going on. To pass the time, I measured my hand against his to see how much bigger it was than mine, and found it was not a lot. His hair seemed a little out of place, so I combed it for a few miles, which helped pass the time—but I could hear my father-in-law's teeth occasionally clacking.

"'George!' he would frequently bark, 'Watch what you're doing!' And for a few miles, you could actually see daylight between us. Then my neck got tired, and the shoulder of your daddy-to-be made such a nice cushion, but that put my mouth so close to his ear that it just begged to be nibbled—and the next thing I knew, I found myself in the backseat next to my new mother-in-law, with my new father-in-law sitting where I had been beside my new husband.

"I wanted to object, but at the time, my feelings toward Lloyd Arnold bordered on pure awe. My daddy wore khakis to his carpentering job, but Lloyd Arnold wore white shirts and a suit most of the time. As a fairly young man, he had cheerfully had his bad teeth pulled, and the dentures never fit very well. But like with every other unpleasant or unexpected event in his life, he simply rattled the change in his pocket, whistled a tune, and got on with the show. But when he was nervous or irritable, he made a clacking sound with his teeth in a way I thought was fascinating.

"He was very typical of the dads of that era—physically present with his family, caring in the crises, but not terribly communicative, especially about his faith. But his children knew they could count on him, and all three loved and respected him.

"As for Margaret Arnold, this was the first time I realized that few thoughts, however fleeting or insignificant, ever passed through her mind without being verbalized. Of course, I was young and self-centered, so the rest of the trip was one of the longest I ever remember taking. I was more than delighted to arrive at the coast to meet all my other new relatives. I hoped beyond hope they were the strong, silent type. They turned out to be very nice people whom I enjoyed, and I felt that their whole world must surely be revolving around us newlyweds.

"They were a table-game family, and we kept a constant game of 42* going on the screened porch. This was one of my favorite things about my new family. We had a grand rivalry, a foretaste of many happy hours I would spend with my in-laws playing 42. Later, they taught us to play bridge.

"The next day we loaded the car to drive over to meet more relatives, planning to stay a few days there before driving back to West Texas. As I recall, it was a 50-mile drive, and the air-conditioning in the car played out about 10 miles down the road, so you can imagine how many times your Grandmother Arnold let us know it was HOT!

"The heat did not, however, dampen her enthusiasm for describing every wildflower growing along the road in minute detail." Then Mother laughed, shaking her head. "I had SO much to learn about relating to a mother-in-law. I wish I had learned more sooner. Ah, well."

She went on with her story. "Just as we pulled into the drive at your great grandmother's apartment, I realized I had left my purse on the screened porch back at the coast. Thought I would die. When I finally got up the nerve to tell my new father-in-law where my purse was, he clacked his teeth, took a swig of antacid, donned his hat, and headed back to the coast. It took only a few short years before he was able to see the humor in it."

We laughed together in the twilight, and I began to see my now frail and tiny grandad in a new light. I tried to imagine him in the power position of a middle-aged man in his prime—and my parents as newlyweds. I wondered if it seemed a long time ago to them. Probably not.

But Mother had done her job well. I did feel better about my own absent-mindedness. It was obviously in my genes!

---

* A game similar to many card games, with bidding and suits, but played with dominoes. It has been called "the national game of Texas."

With renewed patience I began pointing out things of interest to the children as we drove. Daddy joined in because he loved few things better than seeing sights and reading historical markers. As kids, David, Rachel, and I had come to refer to them as "hysterical" markers because, upon seeing one, Daddy often threw on the brakes with such force that the three of us ended up in a pile in the back of the station wagon.

After one final supper stop at Kiddie Burger, where Zach and Zeke let off steam on the playground while I nursed baby Rachel in heavenly peace, we reluctantly piled back into the wagon and headed east with the sunset in our rearview mirror. Barring the unexpected, we would pillow our heads that night in Mother and Daddy's little bungalow in Virginia.

Back in the saddle again, the herd fed and snoozing contentedly, the Trail Boss was ready to hit the asphalt track once again. Nightfall brought with it blessed serenity as starlight illuminated the happy trails stretching out under the headlights of our fully loaded wagon.

Daddy brought a steaming styrofoam cup of coffee to his lips and paused for a quick second to inhale the rich scent before partaking of a sip. After breathing out the "Ahhh" that always follows the first taste of good hot coffee, I'm pretty sure I overheard him whisper softly, "Yeeehaw…let's bring this herd on home. And Lord, would you mind sending a couple of angels to ride shotgun the rest of the way?"

The LORD gave them rest all around…

—JOSHUA 21:44 NKJV

CHAPTER 10

Not My Mother's Thanksgiving

~

Our children were frantic. Thanksgiving was upon us, and that year I'd volunteered to host the event at our home, including stuffing and cooking the turkey and setting an actual cloth-covered table with nondisposable dinnerware.

Rachel, then 17, upon discovering this fact, sat me down in the living room and in her most maternal tone of voice asked, "Mom, do you really think you're mature enough to handle a major holiday that involves actual food preparation?"

I saw her younger brother nod his head in agreement and was forced to admit, with some sense of shock, that my own children were afraid to trust me alone with a frozen Butterball.

"Not to worry," I continued to reassure them. "I know what I'm doing."

And so, when Thanksgiving morning came, I made an attempt—with the help of heaven—to baste with the best of 'em.

I was putting on a brave front, but truth be told, my family had some reason for concern.

I own a T-shirt that says "Martha Stewart Doesn't Live Here." Actually, she probably wouldn't even be tempted to drop by for a visit.

For as long as I can remember, our smoke alarm has served as our family dinner bell. When our now-married son, Zeke, was five years old, I handed him a perfectly browned piece of toast one morning.

Without batting an eye the little guy took the toast—along with his dinner knife—walked to the trash can, and automatically started scraping it.

"Zeke, honey," I said cheerfully, "you don't have to scrape your toast today. Mommy didn't burn it!"

"Oh," he said thoughtfully, glancing down at the toast in surprise. "I thought we always had to whittle our toast."

The tradition of serving blackened food continued in the Freeman kitchen for many more years. When Zachary, my eldest son, was about 13, I recall pulling a charred-past-recognition casserole out of the oven one evening. The alarm was bellowing, the kitchen was soon filled with the familiar fog of fresh smoke. As I set the casserole down on the counter and brushed a damp lock of hair from my forehead, Zach nonchalantly strolled into the kitchen, put his arm around me, and said, "Mmm, mmm, mmm. Smells like Mom's home cookin'!"

A few months ago, Gabe was home from school with a head cold. I took a notion to fry up some bacon for breakfast, so I plopped the bacon in a skillet and set it on the burner (turned to medium high). It was a chilly morning, and soon I got another notion: to take a hot bath to warm myself up. So I immediately retired to the bathroom for a nice long soak. If Gabe had not been home and seen the first few flames leaping from the skillet, my kitchen would have, literally, gone up in smoke.

My problem, I've deduced, is not that I'm a bad cook. It's just that I'm easily distracted. I'm sort of like a middle-aged toddler who finds herself totally fascinated and absorbed with the next new activity—leaving the previous activity (for example, putting something in the oven) erased from all memory.

Over the years, I've often wondered whether my children have grown so accustomed to overcooked food that they might accidentally mistake the charcoal for the chicken at someone else's outdoor barbecue.

~

This past May, a magazine writer wanted to send a photographer down to our house to take pictures of our family enjoying a "typical" Sunday afternoon backyard picnic. I gently explained to the journalist that the sort of food I normally prepare probably shouldn't be photographed except, perhaps, for reading audiences with especially strong stomachs. Surgeons and zookeepers might be okay.

"Not to worry," she said, "we'll hire a professional to come over to your house to cook, decorate the table, and style the food."

"Wow," I said. "That sounds like a DEAL."

And so it came to pass that by the time Jim, the photographer from Chicago, showed up at my door, a professional food stylist and friend, Jane Jarrell, had miraculously turned my backyard picnic table into a *Southern Living*–ish spread. There were fresh wildflowers in hues of bright purple, orange, and yellow peeking merrily over the tops of tall galvanized buckets. Straw placemats that looked like watermelon halves set off hot-pink and green watermelon plates and bright green glasses and utensils. Fresh ripe strawberries and watermelon chunks overflowed from two clear glass bowls in the center of the table, which was festooned by heaping plates of barbecue beef, baked beans, mustard-spiked potato salad, and asparagus pasta. A peach cobbler bubbled away in the oven, its vanilla and cinnamon fragrance tantalizing us even out-of-doors.

My children took one look at the feast—another longing look toward Jane—then turned to me and asked, "Mom, can we keep her? Huh? Please?"

Sadly, Jane had to return to her own family at that point, but I assured Jim and my family that I felt certain I could carry out any remaining hostessing duties—solo.

"Do you make up the stories about the crazy things you do in your books?" Jim asked at one point between snapping pictures of my family deliriously stuffing their faces with Jane's fabulous food.

I shrugged. "To tell you the truth, Jim, so far I haven't had to make up any stories. Weird stuff happens to me almost everyday. It's like writing-material manna from heaven."

I noticed that he looked slightly unconvinced.

The afternoon wore on, and Jim asked to take pictures of us down at the dock on the lake we live by.

As we gathered for photos of our family happily fishing and boating and lounging together, I volunteered to bring some soft drinks down to the lakeside. Conveniently absent from the pictures would be the typical family squabbles, the whining about the heat, and taking our turns accidentally snagging one another in the shins with worm-baited fishhooks.

When I sauntered down the pier with a tray full of refreshments, the jokes commenced.

"Hey Mom!" Gabe hollered in my direction. "Are you sure you can handle serving Dr. Pepper without Jane's help?"

"Yeah," chimed in Jim the photographer, relaxed and feeling almost part of the family at this point. "I hope you can handle pouring drinks into cups without the aid of a professional food stylist and all."

"Very funny," I chirped as I set the tray down on a table.

I picked up a two-liter bottle of Dr. Pepper and heard an ominous fizzing sound from the cap. "Ooops," I said, "it sounds like it might have gotten shaken up as I walked down here. I'd better open it over the LAAAaaaa..."

At which point everything in my world went dark and wet.

When I surfaced, gasping for breath, I saw six startled faces staring down to where I found myself floating next to a large bobbing bottle of Dr. Pepper. I could not believe it. All I had had to do was open a soft-drink bottle and pour a few drinks. A task even the most inexperienced of homemakers (or kindergartners) should be able to handle. Now I suddenly found myself—boots, jeans, dignity, and Dr. Pepper—swimming in the lake.

"Is she all right?" I heard Jim ask my husband.

Scott's response was remarkably laid-back, he having grown accustomed to my mishaps after 25 years. "Oh, yeah," he nodded in my gurgling, gagging, arm-waving direction. "She does this kind of stuff all the time. Go ahead and take some pictures of her before we fish her out. It'll make a great story."

∾

And so perhaps you can now understand why it was with no small sense of trepidation that I mentally geared up to tackle a regulation-sized turkey that Thanksgiving Day.

To help prepare myself for the big moment, I chose to read *The Joy of Cooking* alongside *Feel the Fear and Do It Anyway*.

My grandmother and my mother before me were wonderful cooks, amazing hostesses. I cannot blame my cooking disorder on faulty upbringing or lack of training.

One skill, however, that my mother taught me early on stays with me and continues as a female family tradition: She taught me that part of being a truly beautiful woman is learning to enjoy a good laugh at yourself. (She also taught me to write down the embarrassing or unusual things I do and do it quickly, then re-tell them or write them in journals. Ultimately she helped launch a career in which I now make an actual profit from talking and writing about all the messes I get myself into. We may have a few dysfunctions in our family, but at least we have the creativity to make them sound entertaining.)

Every year, as "we gather together to ask the Lord's blessing," my husband asks each one of us to share something we are thankful for. The holiday I've been telling you about brought statements like, "We are thankful the turkey isn't made from tofu this year." And "We are grateful for fire extinguishers in every room." And thanks from my husband for take-out food and good restaurants.

But for my part, I am thankful for a mother who—though she wasn't able to teach me to be a great cook—taught me the incredible, redemptive power of a good belly laugh.

The Lord has done great things for us; whereof we are glad.

—Psalm 126:2 kjv

The Value of Humor

~

Ironically, I met Joseph Michelli—child psychologist, author, speaker, and proponent of humor—under very humorous circumstances. (In fact, he was preparing to leave the country, clown suit in tow, to cheer up some children in a Russian hospital, along with the more famous Patch Adams.) He was on a Hollywood talk show that I was to appear on as well.

Unfortunately, the producer assumed that Dr. Michelli's wife was ME, and thus, with only minutes until show time, there ensued a Keystone Cops adventure in which I was finally found (standing on the corner, waiting at my hotel for the limo) and rushed to the studio.

After the show, I rode back to the hotel with Dr. and Mrs. Michelli. I immediately knew these parents were the genuine article. They called their kids on their cell phone, talking and laughing and, obviously, sincerely enjoying their parenthood and their children.

I immediately went home and ordered Michelli's book, *Humor, Play & Laughter: Stress-Proofing Life With Your Kids.* How I wish I'd had this book at my bedside when I was a young mother. Here's just a sampling of what humor has been scientifically proven to do for families, according to Dr. Michelli's book!

- Minimize distorted perceptions of danger
- Help manage anger more effectively, thereby reducing conflict

- Provide breathing room for constructive, loving and logical decision-making
- Assist in communicating difficult feelings
- Enhance feelings of well-being
- Augment creativity
- Strengthen social relationships
- Abate the physical ravages of stress
- Create a home environment of warmth and joy

CHAPTER 11

Feathering Our Messy Nests with Memories

~

I love it that my mother-in-law, Beverly, is messy and disorganized. I love it that she has never claimed to be a great cook. It has relieved me of a tremendous amount of pressure in at least one area. Since a can is a can is a can, Scott has never been able to say, "Boy, honey, your green pea soup doesn't taste exactly like my mom's green pea soup."

I have also had the great good fortune to be married to a man whose mother has, for the most part, been a less than enthusiastic housekeeper. Now, when push comes to shove or there's a party coming, Beverly can dust and straighten up and entertain with the best of them. But let's face it, neither she nor I was born a compulsive cleaner. And for better or for worse, my children (her grandchildren) also appear to have been born minus the compulsive-cleaning gene.

For example, my oldest son, Zachary, and I were discussing the family tendency to be messy last night. He told me that at camp one summer his cabin was so sloppy that his roommates had to dig through piles to find doors. He described their plan to appease the Counselor/Room Inspector.

"We put up a sign that said, 'We are too busy practicing godliness to have time for cleanliness.' Then we left him a cold can of soda."

"Did it work?" I asked, impressed.

"Nah. The counselor pointed to the sign and the room and yelled 'BLASPHEMY AND BRIBERY!' at the top of his lungs. But he did drink the Coke."

As with Zachary, Bev and I would love to be able to snap our fingers and have everything fall into place in our living quarters. Bev struggled with guilt over being a "relaxed" homemaker for many years and then, a few years ago, came to her moment of truth. She made the announcement to her family with a mixture of pride and relief.

"I have given housekeeping a good, 25-year try."

Having had an interest in art over the years, Bev then decided to direct her energies into exploring more-creative avenues. Since then I've never had to worry about sprinting around my house, spiffing it up before a visit from Bev. For this fact alone I'm the envy of daughters-in-law the world over.

True to her newly announced goals, Bev became one of those brave women who return to college in midlife. She discovered she excelled especially in the area of photography. Her newfound skill not only brought her creative talents out in the open, but proved to perfectly complement her husband's passion for cross-country motorcycling.

As she and my father-in-law, Jim, explored the nooks and crannies of small-town America, her eyes were ever open for that perfect wildflower or rustic barn to shoot. (With a camera, not a shotgun. In Texas, sometimes these things have to be spelled out.) Because of her skill, we have been privileged to have a "pro" on hand to photograph all major family events. Beverly also inspired me, just before I had my first child, to take a class in photography as one of my college electives. It proved to be one of the most useful courses I've ever taken. As a result, we do not bore our friends with mere "snapshots" of the grand-kids. Though our kitchens may need a good scrubbing, Bev and I think the brag books we have created are aesthetic mar-vels, thank you very much. (As the T-shirt saying goes, "Behind every successful woman is a messy house.")

Lately my mother-in-law has been stretching her wings in the area of watercolor painting. Whatever she still lacks in house-cleaning, she makes up for in the beauty she brings to canvas— though, ever modest, she would beg to differ. She told me of a recent art lesson during which the experienced "professional" teacher bent over her painting and loudly gave his critique.

"'All I can say is LESS, LESS, LESS and BIGGER, BIGGER, BIGGER!'

"I wanted to yell back, 'What exactly does that MEAN, MEAN, MEAN?'" she sighed.

However, Bev must have caught her teacher's meaning because she recently had a very successful show of her own paintings, and she's about to head out on her second trip to Italy, to paint beside her peers in the romantic countryside.

Once again inspired by Bev, I too decided to dabble in paint. Poring over stacks of her *Decorating Ideas* magazines, I came across the old "paint with crumpled newspaper" idea. Let me just say the boys' bedroom walls looked marvelous. So did their woodwork, mirror—and finally, their carpet. When my sons stared at their speckled room in disbelief, I felt I had to come up with an explanation—one they would believe. The answer came to me as a gift.

"It was Grandma's idea," I heard myself say.

How many daughters-in-law have a mother-in-law who insists on leaving the dirty dishes in the sink so she can jump in the lake for a swim or organize a game of croquet with the kids? She's coming out this weekend to teach Gabe to swim, just as she has taught most of her grandchildren. Recently, a good friend of Bev's told me, "I've never met anyone with as much natural talent as Bev, especially when it comes to teaching others a skill."

Beverly has unending patience with those whom she occasionally teaches. On several occasions, she has treated a grandchild to an afternoon of learning to draw on the "right side of the brain." I'd always taught my children not to draw on the walls or the wrong side of a piece of paper, but it never entered my mind they should be taught to draw on the right sides of their brains. Leave it to Grandma...

Though Jim and Bev's kids are grown, they both continued to provide opportunities for us to get together as a family—to make memories. As a memorable example, one spring Jim and Bev invited Scott and his brother, Kent, to come up and join them for a weekend of skiing—encouraging the "boys" with a good opportunity to get away, have some fun, and just hang out together. And there have been motorcycle trips, outings to the Glen Rose Bluegrass Festival, tickets provided to the Harlem Globetrotters, the theater, and the circus. On an outing to a theme park, Jim wore a sweatshirt that read, "I'm Celebrating My 60th Birthday with My Eight Grandchildren at Six Flags Over Texas."

Through all these experiences, Jim and Bev provided fun ways for their adult children and their spouses, and their grandchildren, to enjoy each other's company and, in the process, create warm memories. But there is nothing to quite compare with the celebration of Christmas at the Freemans'.

To Beverly, Christmas isn't Christmas without a minimum of three Christmas trees, a warm hearth, poinsettias, old-fashioned holiday cards, and ivy—a veritable "chestnuts roasting on an open fire" picture. It's important to her to make the season special, especially for her grandchildren. To accomplish that, she always arranges something unique—a genuine "memory maker"—each season.

One year she wrote a letter to each of the grandchildren about a memory she had of Christmases from her childhood and read them each aloud as we were gathered around the tree. Last year we began our Christmas Eve morning at the ice-skating rink at Tandy Center in downtown Fort Worth. Her daughter and daughters-in-law may have been too faint of heart to attempt the ice ("We're getting too old!"), but Grandma Bev was out there skating among her eight grandchildren as if this were what all grandmothers do.

When we returned to her exquisitely decorated home, there was even more fun in store. A few days before Christmas, Bev and I scripted a play that would involve each of the eight grandchildren. Bev came up with the theme—acknowledging our ancestral roots in the celebration of Christmas (in this case, our roots in Sweden). She had suggested the format, too—a talk show. As the kids acted out a variety of characters during the actual performance, the raw talent oozing from our prodigies was almost palpable.

Once the comedy was over, the children wound things down, and we moved to a more serious scene. Heather, the oldest female of the grandkids, carried out a Christmas tradition from Sweden. Wearing a long-skirted Christmas dress, her hair wreathed with a garland, she sang "Silent Night" for her family audience. (We had discussed decorating the garland in her hair with lighted candles, but my reputation for creating spontaneous combustion at Christmas gatherings kept us in check.)

Following Heather's solo, Rachel Praise and Cousin Hartley joined in a rendition of "Away in a Manger." Then it fell to Scott, the Freeman Christmas storyteller, to come up with an authentic-sounding tale about a special Christmas in the Old Country. He didn't disappoint us, coming out with accents and gestures and facial expressions that held the children spellbound.

After the show, we gathered for the grand finale, a scrumptious smorgasbord of Swedish meatballs with all the trimmings. As we sat down at the festive table, Jim thanked the Lord for keeping us together as a family, and for the greatest gift of all—His Son.

~

On the first Easter after Scott and I were married, my mother gave us a copy of Edith Schaeffer's book *What Is a Family?* It's been one of the most significant books I've ever read, and it has continued to shape my own desire to put my family at the top of my life's priorities, difficult as that is in these hectic times in which we live. I've referred to Mrs. Schaeffer's writing again and again over the years, with so many sentences marked that—in the tradition of my father—practically the entire book is underlined. One of my favorite chapters is entitled "A Museum of Memories."

Mrs. Schaeffer believes that every family deposits memories into a "family museum"—some good, some painful. In the case of my own little family, my parents, and my in-laws, we have all—on various occasions—deposited both kinds. But even the bad memories, when looked at in a certain light, can be redeemed. It was a comfort to read Edith's description of her husband, the esteemed Dr. Francis Schaeffer, and the infamous potted ivy.

Mrs. Schaeffer writes, "When a flare of temper would strike Fran like a cyclone, he'd lift up this red clay pot and heave the ivy on the floor." The ivy had been swept up and re-potted so many times over the years that it became a family joke. In her maternal way of communicating, Mrs. Schaeffer went on to say something else I've never forgotten:

> When some new little family is frightened of the
> emotions of anger, disappointment, disgust, or

dismay because of what one or the other has done, the remembrance of the ivy can remind both the calm one and the upset one, "This doesn't need to be the end; just think how many times the ivy was thrown, and how many times it all got cleaned up and re-potted. Our human relationship can continue to get better and stronger just as the plant continued to grow with a sturdy, healthy growth".... There will be both good and disturbing memories which will help your children to have a realistic understanding of human beings, of life in a fallen world where sin continues to spoil things, and of the fact that there can be a rebuilding after an "earthquake," and that it is *worth it all* to go back and make a new start.

Isn't that a comfort? There is no family who has a museum of picture-perfect memories, of course, but I want to encourage myself and others to continue making deliberate efforts, to make the sacrifice of time and energy, to use some of the time we have left on this earth to fill our family's museum with wonderful, happy memories. Mrs. Schaeffer comments, "Someone in the family—one who is happily making it his or her career, or both parents, perhaps a grandparent or two... at least one person needs to be conscious that memories are important, and that time can be made to have double value by recognizing that what is done today will be tomorrow's memory."

Memories aren't just events that happen once and disappear into the atmosphere. They are embedded in the backs of our minds, affecting how we function, think, feel and make decisions. How very thankful I am to both sets of my children's grandparents for purposefully, often sacrificially, making it a priority to create good memories for their adult children and grandkids.

In the case of my husband's mother, Beverly, I personally hope that her efforts to make fun memories will always take precedence over old dull housekeeping. Besides, I (and Bev too, I'm sure) agree wholeheartedly with something I saw at the mall recently, written on a lavender T-shirt worn by a modern granny—"Housework makes you ugly." After all, what will the family most remember? A perfectly scrubbed home—or a museum of memories?

An empty stable stays clean—
but there is no income from an empty stable.
—Proverbs 14: 4 TLB

I dedicate this chapter to my beloved father-in-law, Jim Freeman, who passed away after a short bout with cancer. His funeral—on April 22, 2002—reflected his life. The chapel was filled with church friends, businessmen, an aisle of his teenage grandkids, and at least two rows of motorcyclists dressed in riding gear. (He was comfortable in any crowd…) Jim was 70 and had completed his last ride only a few short weeks before. Songs at the service ranged from his favorite Willie Nelson version of "On the Road Again," to "Amazing Grace," and finally, to a revised version of "I'll Fly Away"—"I'll Ride Away." Beverly, my mother-in-law, was a living watercolor of courage, beauty, and grace during those weeks. When she stood to receive the ceremonial flag from the military men at the burial site, I felt more proud of her in that moment than at any other time in my life.

A lifetime of memories added up to a day, a life, and a legacy we will always cherish.

CHAPTER 12

Irregular Relatives

On a quiet afternoon when my three older kids were in school and Gabe was out chasing bullfrogs in the sunshine, the quiet was broken by the shrill ring of the phone. Mother's voice on the other end of the wire sounded tense.

"Becky, I've had a call from Aunt Hazel," she said. "Are you sitting down? Grandmother Arnold has been diagnosed with Alzheimer's disease!"

After the first wave of shock and sadness, my internal reaction to Mother's announcement was, *So that's what's been wrong!* I couldn't help wondering how many years this had been developing. How much of my paternal grandmother's self-centeredness and the temper tantrums had really been beyond her control?

As it turned out, my very patient, upbeat grandfather had been keeping much of what was going on with them to himself. He had spent a lifetime protecting his wife, looking after her. Though we all stood amazed at his fortitude, it was apparent that he truly loved her.

"The last time they were here, I couldn't believe what their life together had become," Mother shared. "Margaret could not sit still longer than a couple of minutes at a time, but she also couldn't get up and down by herself. 'Honey!' she would holler, 'I gotta get up. Help me up!' And frail as he was, Grandaddy would haul himself out of his chair, take her hands, and pull her to her feet. She'd wander through the house five minutes or so, sit down for two, and then repeat the process."

"Bless his heart," I empathized. "I had no idea Grandad was taking on so much. Have you noticed her deteriorating?"

"Well, I remember taking them shopping one day not long ago. Your grandmother picked out a ceramic mallard duck she wanted to buy and stepped up to the counter to pay for it. In the end, she had to give me her purse to sort out the right amount of money for it. It was so sad, but yet she was determined to do it, almost as if she were trying to prove to herself she was still okay."

"Reminds me of the bumper sticker that says, 'I shop, therefore I am,'" I concluded.

Mother laughed in agreement. "Anyway, it appears the two of them were living on canned vegetable soup, and Lloyd was exhausted from lack of sleep. Still, he didn't tell anyone. But then his back began to go out on him, and eventually they both were on the floor and couldn't get up. Interestingly, it was your grandmother who managed to crawl to the phone and dial a friend."

My Aunt Hazel and Uncle Buddy had agreed to take Grandmother and Grandaddy into their home to care for them. A few weeks later, Mother shared that one morning grandmother had come into Aunt Hazel's kitchen and announced, "That man in my bed is not my husband!" Hazel gently put her arm around grandmother and replied, "Well, let's look at it this way, Margaret. How many women your age have that kind of problem to worry about?"

Mother continued. "We have to take laughter whenever and wherever we can get it, or we may find ourselves making pottery in an asylum." She sighed. "How I wish I had been more patient with her through the years!"

"Oh, Mom, you couldn't have known," I insisted. "No one could handle grandmother for long without wanting to ask her if she was up for a rousing round of The Quiet Game."

When my mother had agreed to marry my father, she thought Margaret Arnold was so sweet she could have eaten her with a spoon. Six months later, she wished she had. My grandmother made most of the major mistakes it's possible for a mother-in-law to make. She talked about one daughter-in-law to the other and then reversed the process. When grandbabies began arriving, she informed my mom in her cutest baby-talk voice, "I the Going Grandmother. *Your* mother the Baby-sitting Kind."

As is true with so many people suffering from personality or mental disorders, Grandmother grew worse with age. At one point she became so volatile and created such a tense atmosphere when she visited in our home that my parents just about stopped having her come. She became more and more unreasonable, self-centered, and demanding—and the talking never stopped. To our wonderment, she even talked through the night in her sleep! The first few minutes after our grandmother would go home, our family would just sit, rather numb, staring into space, savoring the silence.

~

Most of us have at least one relationship with another family female that is, shall we say, *sticky*. Mothers-in-law and moms are often at the top of that list. What to do with these difficult relationships that we can't avoid? Mom gave me a book that had helped her immensely in learning to accept and deal with her own mother-in-law. The title? *Irregular People*.

In the book, Joyce Landorf Heatherly explains that almost everyone has at least one person in their life who truly makes living one continuous pain in the derriere. What heightens the pain is that this person is not a mere acquaintance of ours. No, unfortunately it is more complicated than that, for we are usually related to them, either by birth or by marriage. Heatherly writes, "It's so frustrating…because you can't reason with them, can't depend on them, and can't expect any real support from them. We must perceive our irregular person as perhaps 'permanently handicapped.' It is the only avenue to take towards acceptance and healing."

If this person happens to be a very close relative, the reality that you have an irregular, probably *unchangeable* person in your life is an enormous loss that has to actually be grieved. The idea of irregular people helped Mother get some emotional distance from the inner hurt she often felt from her mother-in-law's insensitive remarks.

"When I think of the hours I wasted standing at the kitchen sink, doing dishes and mentally stewing about our latest tiff!" Mother mused one afternoon. "She was a woman who desperately longed for intimacy, but for whatever reasons, she seemed locked inside a dome of self—the worst form of solitary confinement! She could see people, but she couldn't seem to mesh comfortably with them. And now I wonder if there has not always been some chemical or emotional problem that overwhelmed her. In hindsight, I suspect she did the best she could in life."

My mom's input has been invaluable to me as I myself have struggled to deal with the irregular people who have come across my own path. When I was a pre-teen suffering from a tough day in the lunchroom with mean-spirited kids, my mother told me to always remember that "hurting people hurt people." The knowledge didn't erase all of the pain, but at least I didn't blame myself or think less of who I was when others were cruel or unfeeling. Truly, the people who have the hardest time loving others are unbelievably hard on themselves. Usually, their mind is a place you wouldn't want to go into alone. I just finished talking on the phone with a dear friend of mine whose mother is borderline narcissistic, a mental disorder many therapists feel is one of the saddest and most resistant to treatment. Narcissistics inflict amazing emotional pain on the people who try to love them because they are truly incapable of giving real love.

"How did you come to peace with your mother's cruel words?" I asked.

My friend replied, "Well, a year or two of counseling plus an antidepressant helped. But what helped the most was when the counselor met my mother and talked with her for one session. When Mom left the room, the therapist called me in and said, 'Honey, you need to go ahead and start grieving the loss of a good, whole, and healthy mother. Your mom will never be this for you. In your case, I would recommend that you build a life as far apart from her as possible—or you may not be able to survive emotionally.'"

Hers is a sad and extreme case of dealing with an irregular mother. But some of you reading this book may be in just such a situation. Thankfully, my friend's mother-in-law took on the nurturing, caring role of a mother figure in her life.

After Mother and I had discussed Landorf's book and its significance to this chapter, she ventured, "So, Becky, I was just wondering…"

"Don't worry. The answer is no."

"No what?"

"No, you are not *irregular*. You are most certainly certifiably *crazy*, but you are not irregular."

"Whew. What a relief."

My heartfelt prayer, along with my mother's, is that you will experience the *relief* that comes with accepting that some people in your life are simply, irrevocably *irregular*. If they have hurt you again and again in ways you cannot comprehend, repeat to yourself, "This is not about me. This is not about me." Then let go of stewing, fixing them, and trying to please them. Psychologists tell us that peace and freedom usually follow on the heels of *relinquishing our expectations*, especially in dysfunctional relationships.

If you prefer a shortcut over long-term therapy, I have found that it helps to have a closet you can run to where you keep a huge plastic bat to beat the living daylights out of a feather pillow while screaming, "I'm going NUTS! She's driving me CRAZY! Really, Lord, I can't TAKE it anymore!" Then once you have exhausted your anger, wipe your brow, straighten your hair, and walk out, refreshed and revived, ready to face your irregular person again—who will no doubt point out the tired look in your eyes, the weight you appear to have gained, and mess you've just made of your closet.

Be kind and compassionate to one another,
forgiving one another, just as in Christ God forgave you.

—Ephesians 4:32

Don't Take It Personally

~

A physician is not angry at the intemperance
of a mad patient, nor does he take it ill to be railed at
by a man in fever. Just so should a wise man
treat all mankind, as a physician does his patient,
and look upon them only as sick and extravagant.

—SENECA

Learning to handle hurts, wounds and disappointments more skillfully will not stop things from
going wrong in life. People may still be unkind, and
random events can still hurt you....What will
change, however, is the space you rent them in your
mind and the amount of anger, hopelessness, and
despair you feel. I cannot emphasize this point too
strongly. Life may not be perfect, but you can learn
to suffer less.

—DR. FRED LUSKIN, FROM *FORGIVE FOR GOOD*

CHAPTER 13

A Pocketful of Forgiveness

~

On the way home from a family reunion, it occurred to me to wonder about Mother's daddy, my Grandaddy Jones, who had died when I was in late grade school. I remembered him as an elderly fellow always dressed in khakis who had a fascinating workshop in his garage and seemed to love for us children to visit him there to explore it. The relationship between him and my folks had seemed warm, but I had picked up from remarks among the Jones family that their early life with him had not been easy.

Mother had promised to tell me about this, and when she did, I thought the story worth the retelling. So many grown daughters struggle to forgive a less-than-perfect parent. As one of the female Story-Keepers in our family, I value these real-life lessons even more than old photographs. In my mother's own words, this is that story...

~

In our home, we had lots of fun lots of the time, and if my father had not had a serious problem, it would have been fun most of the time.

Daddy was a true eccentric who, in his twilight years, flatly refused to pay a barber to cut his hair and did it himself. He merely grabbed a topknot of faded auburn hair, held it straight up, and then shaved all the hair around the edge. Once he brushed the topknot down over the shaved area, it actually didn't look too bad.

When he developed a toothache, he refused to pay the dentist. He tied a string around the offending tooth, tied the other end of the string around the bumper of their 1930-model car (in 1970), and tried to persuade Nonnie to drive the car down the alley behind their house. Pliable as she was, she turned him down.

I thank God for the good memories I do have of him. The best are from my preschool years, I think. He was a nice-looking fellow, as I remember, and seemed ten feet tall when he swung me up to his shoulders for a ride. I'd sit by the side of the dirt road leading to our house out in the country, piling mounds of sandy red soil on top of my bare feet until I spied him coming over the hill after work. I'd run to meet him, and on the way to the house would get to view the world from atop his broad shoulders.

He would have walked home from a ten-hour day at his job as a carpenter, his fair skin burned red from working under a blazing sun all day. The Great Depression was just ending, and his pay was pitifully low. I was his seventh child.

Most evenings he stretched out on his bed with the daily paper and let me comb, braid, and pin-curl his wavy auburn hair. And if the evening was really warm, he might stretch out on the bare wood floor in front of an open door to catch the evening breeze. My brother Genie would lie on one of his outstretched arms, and I on the other, while he told us wonderful stories. A favorite of mine was about his imaginary Other Family who lived off in the wilds, and I never doubted for a minute it was true. The mother was a wild woman who roamed through the prairie with a passel of kids, all barely clothed, howling like a banshee in the wind. Here he would do a wonderful imitation that fairly set my hair on end. This was so real to me that I began to save pennies so he could buy clothes for them on his next trip to visit them. When Genie told me Daddy was just making it up, I felt as if I'd lost part of my family!

But then an evening came when he appeared to me to be sick at the supper table. I must have been about five years old, and I always sat on a bench between Genie and Lloyd, the two youngest of the five brothers. Daddy seemed terribly sleepy that night, and he stumbled when he walked. And his table manners were terrible. I remember it being awfully quiet during the meal, as Nonnie moved around the table to serve us. Her face was sad, and she said almost nothing. Only later did I learn that his tiredness and clumsiness came from a bottle.

After that, there were many times when we went through long periods of his drinking, and with that drinking came violent outbursts of temper when the older kids had it pretty rough. Sometimes Nonnie took the brunt of it. Over the years, I suppose each one of the seven of us had at least one encounter with him when we actually did hand-to-hand combat.

Because of his drinking bouts, he was often unable to work, or else there was no carpentry work to be had in our small town. So of course there was never enough money, and we were always among the poor people of the town. When each of us kids grew old enough to work, we took our turns helping to put red beans, milk gravy, and fried potatoes on the table. Gradually, a blazing rage and hatred against him settled in me, and even after he stopped drinking when I was in high school, I would hardly stay in the same room with him.

Nonnie always made sure we kids went to church with her every Sunday, and even though it was pretty legalistic, we certainly grew up knowing right from wrong. I had a strong moral sense that served me well as a teenager, but no personal acquaintance with God Himself, so there was no little self-righteousness in my attitude toward my father.

Daddy was a recluse, and spent hours in his old workshop in the garage. We most often managed to have a great time when he would leave the house. He stopped taking his meals with the family somewhere along the way and stayed in his bedroom, so we were free to laugh, talk, and cut up together at meals. My brother George, the oldest, bought the old house we were living in with a GI loan, and he was a strong presence among us. He often announced supper by yelling, "Soup's on! All feet on the floor and no stabbing above the wrist!" This would precipitate a near-stampede because, at one time, nine of us gathered regularly around our supper table.

Later on, when I began to court a fellow also named George, it complicated matters, but my life turned a lot sweeter, any way you look at it. Nonnie was as hospitable as my father was inhospitable, and in spite of our poverty, she could somehow come up with meals for our friends who didn't mind visiting the unpainted old house on the edge of the highway, even with cars and trucks whizzing by day and night. And George Arnold, who lived in a little white house not nearly as close to the railroad tracks, didn't even seem to notice.

Nonnie was always a great comfort to me throughout some very tough years. She brought light into the gloomy house just by being in it. We all loved and respected her for her gentle ways and would never have hurt her on purpose, so there were not too many wild oats sown, even by her five sons. She got us through it all somehow.

Of course the boys loved to have belching contests, which set my sister Etta's nerves on edge worse than just about anything else they could have done. Usually at least one of them would, after finishing a meal, stand and belch 'til the roof rattled, give a horselaugh, and run down the hallway with her in hot pursuit. Uncle Genie tried it one day, though, and she changed her tactics. As he turned to run, she took her dinner fork and flipped it at him, not really meaning to hit him. The fork stood straight up in the calf of his leg! She was as shocked as he was, and helped bandage him. As the second oldest child, she helped get Lloyd, Genie, and me through high school before moving away on her own.

Since I was the youngest, I spent my senior year in high school in a home that had grown awfully quiet since the older ones had made their way into the world. It was quiet, that is, until your Grandaddy Jones and I would lock horns. He was sober by those years, and it had been a long time since any of us had needed to be afraid of him.

But it was a little late in life to make a new start, so there was never really enough money to take a deep breath. I worked from junior-high age on, just as we all had done. I resented him, and all the lost years, so he and I frequently said blistering things to each other and stormed in and out of rooms, slamming doors until the entire house shook and Nonnie put her fingers in her ears. This was the state of our relationship when I left home to marry George Arnold.

We moved to Lubbock so George could go to Texas Tech, and I missed Nonnie terribly that first year. We went home almost every weekend to visit in the old ramshackle house where they were still living. When I would come into the room where my father was, I expected him to leave it. And he did. I was still so furious with him that I failed to notice he was no longer fighting me. He simply did what I expected him to do, which was to stay out of my way. And then one day, in the space of five minutes, everything changed.

We had been home for the weekend and were loading up one Sunday afternoon to go back to Lubbock. I went to the car to load my overnight bag and stepped back up onto the front porch, planning to go back into the house and hug Nonnie goodbye. As I looked into the hallway, I saw my dad walk by

Nonnie and say something to her I couldn't hear. He put his hand into her apron pocket and then passed on to his bedroom. She came out onto the porch with a strange look on her face, reached into her pocket, and handed me a five-dollar bill.

"Daddy asked me to give this to you and tell you it's part of what he owes you," she said carefully, as if she didn't quite know what my reaction would be.

At first I was shocked. He was such a proud man, and there had been so much anger between us. I had never known him to humble himself before anyone. I don't remember what I said to Nonnie, but I got into the car with George and we drove back to Lubbock. By the time I got there, all traces of anger and bitterness toward my dad had disappeared. I immediately sat down and wrote him a long letter telling him so.

At the time, I didn't realize what a miracle had taken place in him and in me. I think of my relationship with God back then as "long-distance," and it would be several years yet before I knew the reality of His love and presence in my life. Of course, once we come to recognize the presence of God in our lives, we're able to look back and see very clearly how He was working, but at the time, I took the very wonderful change in my emotions as a normal thing. Daddy was sorry for what he had done, and I was glad—very glad—that we were friends again.

And the next time we made a trip home, he was watching at the front door for us. He gave me a big hug and spent the weekend talking our ears off.

From that point on, he always seemed childishly happy to see us, and then when our babies began arriving, he was glad to send Nonnie to stay with us until I was well on my feet again, though I know he missed her.

I've often wondered what my life might have been like if I had tried to live it with hatred in my heart against my dad. Even with our reconciliation, I had more than enough to deal with as an adult living with the consequences of so many years with an alcoholic father. I'm so glad he found a way he could bring himself to say, "I'm sorry, Ruthie."

Years later—after my father died—when I came to know the reality of Christ's presence in my life, He gradually and gently led me to see that I had some things to apologize for, too. My rage and bitterness as a teenager toward Daddy were certainly natural, but I'm not proud of them. Christ cares about everything that happens to us, but He also cares about how we react to them. His desire is to enable us to react as He would—supernaturally.

Of course, as human beings, and especially as adults who have been hurt while children, it goes against our grain to look at our own shortcomings in such situations. Did I not have a right, after all, to my anger?

It may not make much sense, but a lot of Christ's commandments are complete opposites of our natural inclinations. "Love your enemies." "Do good to those who hate you," and so on. The odd thing is that His way works amazingly well. So I owned up to my failures—the hurtful ways I reacted to my father's faults—and asked forgiveness. Of course my father was already gone by then, so I asked God for that forgiveness. And knowing that I am forgiven has given me a sense of peace when I look at the past…

I'm just very thankful to God that I was reconciled to my dad before he died. It's made a great difference.

≈

I couldn't help wondering how much of Mother's very obvious joy in life depended on that simple gesture—the one my grandfather had made when he slipped a five-dollar bill into Nonnie's pocket to pass on to his angry daughter. It wasn't much money, but then, he didn't have much. But oh, the wealth he was able to give his daughter—and her future family—that day!

> *Honour thy father and mother;*
> *(which is the first commandment with promise;)*
> *That it may be well with thee,*
> *and thou mayest live long on the earth.*
>
> —EPHESIANS 6:2-3 KJV

"Forgiveness" Is Flying Above Your Right to a Grievance

~

Doing an injury puts you below your enemy: Revenging one makes you but even with him; Forgiving it sets you above him.

> —BENJAMIN FRANKLIN,
> FROM *POOR RICHARD'S ALMANAC*

CHAPTER 14

Out to Lunch

~

The phone rang, interrupting my thought just before I could capture it on my computer screen. *Oh, pooh,* I said to myself, *I might not get another one today!* As soon as I heard the voice on the other end of the line, however, all irritation vanished. The caller was Shawn, one of my dearest friends. Soon we were both giggling, but I heard a sigh of exhaustion from her as well.

"Becky, I need to laugh. Can we have lunch this week?" she asked. For myself and for most women I know, lunching and laughing has been the cure-all for the occasional blue funk, replacing the therapeutic "buying a new hat" our grandmothers used. I jumped on the invitation like a duck on a june bug.

"Yes! I need a break, big-time. Listen, I went to this little tea room in Arlington called the—oh, shoot—what was it called? It was English-sounding. Winsome? Winded? Windsor! Yes, I think it's called the Windsor Something. Why don't I call and make reservations and see if Brenda can join us?"

Does every woman have friends she just CAN'T WAIT to see so she can tell them the "latest"? I know that my first attempts to write humor would probably never have material- ized if I hadn't enjoyed the camaraderie of my girlfriends over the years. They almost made me long for wild things to happen so I could come to the luncheon table on an equal footing, bringing with me the kind of stories we had all come to expect from each other—stories to make us lay our heads on the table and beat it helplessly with our fists, lost in silent mirth; stories so hilarious we had to hold on to each other's arms to keep from falling out of our chairs right there in the restaurant.

Early in our friendship Brenda had summed up the feelings of us all when she blurted out, "I LOVE to laugh." It reminded me of the song and the scene from the movie *Mary Poppins* where Mary's gentleman friend and the children float to the top of the room because they are laughing so uncontrollably. Now honestly, wouldn't it be a kick if that were really possible? When I get to heaven, one of the things I'm counting on is getting to laugh upside-down on the ceiling of my mansion.

But back to my greatly anticipated lunch date with Brenda and Shawn. It proved to be a day well worth waiting for. I pulled my station wagon up in the parking lot first, followed by Brenda. It suddenly hit me that we'd been friends for 17 years. But then, like minds have a way of clicking together right away and then hanging on to each other for dear life through the years.

Once inside that beautiful restaurant, Brenda and I settled into our chairs, placed the melon-colored napkins in our laps, and sipped our water from crystal goblets with slices of lime floating in them. The restaurant had not opened for lunch until 11:15. This was a late start. If it had opened earlier, I might have set our lunch date to begin at 8:30, just to make sure we had plenty of talking time. I was the first out of the starting blocks.

"So, Brenda, tell me about your new house and your new nursing job."

"Wa-ell," Brenda drawled in her wonderful southern accent, "I made 98 on my nursing exam yesterday. They said it was the highest score they'd ever seen. And then a few minutes later I couldn't figure out how to get a piece of plastic medical equipment apart, and the head nurse had to tell me it was all one piece. Becky, how can I be so smart and act like such a dingbat?"

Ah, a girl after my own heart. There aren't many of us. The tried. The true. The women who could show you their Honor Society cards in their wallets, if only they could remember where they last placed their purse. With Brenda, I can relax.

Shawn joined us, only one hour late. The three of us allow one hour plus or minus for our scheduled appointment times, so Brenda and I never worried that she might not show up. As I had done with Brenda, I did a quick tally of the 20-plus years Scott and I have known Shawn. She and Scott had actually grown up on the same block as kids. An old friend—a rare blessing.

We giggled our way through the wild field salad, the Southwestern crepes, and enough iced tea to drown lesser ladies. Then came dessert, the main course as far as we were concerned. We settled on the tiramisú—with three forks for one serving of an Italian cake that is expensive both in dollars and calories. And seeing the cake, I was reminded of a dream I had had the night before, a real doozy. I couldn't wait to see how the girls might interpret it.

"Okay, now don't make fun of me," I began. However, the corners of their mouths were already starting to turn up. "In my dream, I was sitting in this nice restaurant having lunch with a balding Richard Dreyfuss. I noticed that Richard had a slice of chocolate cheesecake and a cup of coffee set before him. Oh, how I wanted a piece of that cheesecake too, but I was too embarrassed to ask for one. Then the waiter suddenly started singing 'Happy Birthday' to me in French and brought me a whole chocolate cheesecake. I was thrilled. I now had my excuse to eat my favorite dessert.

"But before I could take a bite, my teeth started coming loose and began falling out. So I did the best I could under bad circumstances: I began picking my teeth out of my mouth, first one-by-one, and then several at a time, laying them on my plate. I looked over at Richard Dreyfruss and shrugged, not knowing exactly what to say, and grinned a toothless grin. Mind you, I still had as my main goal finding a way to eat my cheesecake. "Much to my relief, Mr. Dreyfuss put me completely at ease. He loosened his belt a notch and let this previously concealed, humongous belly roll outward, accompanying this with a sigh of relief. Then he said, 'As long as you're getting comfortable by taking out your teeth, I guess I can relax, too. Let's dig in!' So I happily gummed my cheesecake and woke up laughing."

That story opened up the second half of lunch, and by the time I left the restaurant, it was 2:20. I couldn't believe that three hours had flown by so quickly. I felt deeply refreshed, ready to face Real Life again.

I'm convinced we would save enormous amounts of money on counseling and therapy in this country if more people would simply go out to lunch on a regular basis—preferably with friends who are also a little "out to lunch." And some cheesecake now and then won't hurt either. It'll taste good even if your lunch date unexpectedly happens to be Richard Dreyfuss and all your teeth fall out on the table.

There is a friend who sticks closer than a brother.
—Proverbs 18:24

Lunch + Laughter + Loyalty = Friendship

～

Among those whom I like or admire, I can find no
common denominator; but among those whom I
love, I can: All of them make me laugh.
—W.H. Auden

CHAPTER 15

Mother–Daughter Getaway!

~

I received a call from my publisher in Nashville asking me to come speak at their sales conference. I thought this would be the perfect opportunity for a little mother–daughter getaway. Rachel looked dubious. "Mom, are you sure you can get both of us to the airport and get a rental car and follow a map and all?"

"Yes, Rachel," I responded, a little hurt by her lack of confidence in her ol' mom. "And this may come as a shock, but I can comb my own hair and tie my own shoes, too."

We landed in Nashville without a hitch, and in this city, rich in history, Rachel opted to spend the day at the Great American Outlet Mall. We must have spent five hours shopping that day, missing nary a nook, cubby, or cranny. Had an absolute ball at that mall.

That is, until the sun went down and the air grew nippy, our stomachs began growling, and our feet begged for relief— and I realized I'd lost the key to the rental car. An hour-and-a-half after re-tracing our every step—up nooks, around cubbies, and down crannies—we finally found the precious keys in the corner of a remote dressing room.

"Mom," Rachel said, her voice trembling from cold and fatigue as we walked to the car, "you are going to give me gray hair before I'm 14."

In an effort to cheer her up I purchased a pizza and two coloring books, along with a new box of crayons, on the way to the hotel. That night we sat on our beds in our fluffy robes, watching *Touched by an Angel* and a charming movie called *A Thousand Men and a Baby*. I glanced over at Rachel's side of the room and couldn't help noting that her clothes were folded as neatly as little party sandwiches. Even her toiletries were aligned in ascending and descending order.

"Rach," I said, "your side of the room looks like it's been touched by an angel."

She glanced over at the pile of clothes on my bed and replied, "Mom, it looks like a thousand men and a baby had a party on your side of the room!"

Before we knew it, it was time to return to Texas. While we were standing at the ticket counter in the Nashville airport I looked down and noticed that my suitcase had just—exploded! The zipper had popped off, and my clothes were poofing out of the seams and landing around my feet. (If you want to mortify a teenage girl, stand next to her in a nice airport with your underwear lying on the floor around you.)

I ended up having to patch up the suitcase with a roll of duct tape the ticket agent handed to me. (You know you're a redneck if you latch your Samsonite with duct tape…) Rachel disappeared at this point.

Finally I found her, and we flew home to Dallas, retrieved our luggage—both the latched items and the duct-taped ones—and began searching for my car in the parking lot.

This turned out to be more difficult than planned, and after about 30 minutes of huffing and puffing through aisles of parked cars, I went into survival mode.

"Rachel, you sit here with the suitcases," I ordered. "I'll run up and down and look for our car."

On one return trip I noticed Rachel munching on a cookie as she sat staring morosely into space atop our pile of luggage. "Where'd you get that?" I asked.

"A lady came by and said, 'Hon, you look like you could use a cookie.'" With fire in her eyes, Rachel continued, "Mom! She thought I was HOMELESS."

Eventually we found the car. Delighted to be headed home after our long ordeal, we belted ourselves into the front seats, and I turned the key in the ignition.

Nothing.

"Oops," I said quietly. "Guess I left the lights on all weekend. The battery appears to be somewhat dead."

At this point Rachel's chin began to quiver—and I had to get tough.

"Hey, Rach! Buck up! We're Thelma and Louise, remember? Why, we are a pair of brave women, like Helen Keller and Annie Sullivan!"

"Mom," she said flatly, all expression gone from her eyes, "give it up. We're Dumb and Dumber."

By the time we got from Nashville to our home in Greenville, it was 3 A.M. We could have easily driven home from Tennessee in the same amount of time it took us to actually fly, walk, search and run, wait for the airport police, get recharged, and drive home. Oh, let's be frank: We probably could have crawled home and made better time.

A mere 48 hours or so after our return, Rachel actually began speaking to me again.

～

By the end of her eighth-grade year, Rachel had forgotten most of the indignities she'd suffered at my hand, and she allowed me to help her prepare for her middle-school graduation. In her small school district, these graduations are mighty big deals, occasions filled with pomp and circumstance and prom-style party dresses. They are exact replicas of high-school graduations, only the girls are much taller than most of the boys.

Lone Oak Middle School's graduation ceremony was held in the gymnasium. I sat at the top of the bleachers with Scott and our sons and both sets of grandparents to watch our beautiful daughter walk across the stage for her diploma. We'd spent the day finding the perfect dress—gauzy and feminine, lilac flowers on a backdrop of cream—and I'd fixed her auburn curls in a Victorian-style upsweep. Naturally, I'd brought along a camera so I could capture this special moment on film for all time.

"Scott," I whispered, just before our daughter was to rise and walk up for her diploma, "I want to get a close-up of Rachel. I'm going to sneak down to the bottom of the bleachers real quietly and snap a photo."

Just then, a recording of "You'll Never Walk Alone" began playing. (Our school is too small for a genuine choir. We rely on boom boxes to carry us through these traditional proceedings.) I swallowed a lump in my throat as I stood and began to walk down the steps. The words of the song spoke of walking through storms, holding your head high…

I thought of all the storms my daughter and I had braved together over the years, and I couldn't help mouthing the words as I slipped closer toward Rachel, camera in hand—words about not being afraid of darkness but looking forward to the end of the storm, and to a song—

Thump, thump, thump, thump, thump, thump. CLUNK. "OUCH!"

I'd tripped and fallen down about seven steps, reaching the bottom of the bleachers in a final, most undignified thud. My ankle was bleeding, my camera was lying on the ground, every eye was turned in my direction. I gave a brave little wave, reached for my camera, and snapped a picture of my daughter, who was staring into the lens like a deer caught in the headlights.

All around me I heard people whispering.

"Was that Rachel's mother?"

"Is she okay?"

"Isn't she the one who writes those funny books?"

"Didn't she fall off the fence at Zeke's football game?"

With as much dignity as I could muster, I ignored the whispers, ascended the steps with the grace of a princess, and took my place back among the family.

"That was touching," Scott murmured. "I'm sure Rachel will always remember it."

"My ankle is bleeding," I countered, hoping to milk some sympathy out of him.

"Poor Peeky," he replied softly, gently putting a hanky over my wound.

I forced myself to look up again. To my great relief and surprise, Rachel was smiling and laughing and shaking her head. She appeared to be taking my public fall in stride.

Later that evening, at her graduation slumber party, I poked my head into the room full of pajama-clad middle-school graduates.

"Hi, girls," I said. "Are you having fun?"

"Yeah, we're having a blast, Mrs. Freeman."

"Uh, Rachel—do you forgive me for humiliating you?"

"Mom," Rachel answered sweetly, rising to give me a hug. "I don't get embarrassed as much anymore. You made me laugh, and everyone thought it was hilarious. Besides, you did land gracefully—and you got up and went back to your seat really fast."

As I bid the girls goodnight and pulled the door closed behind me, I couldn't help thinking, *My daughter is raising me well.*

The steps of a good man are ordered by the LORD:
and he delighteth in his way. Though he fall, he shall not be
utterly cast down: for the LORD upholdeth him with his hand.

— PSALM 37:23-24 KJV

Mom & Daughter's Best Traveling Tip: Humor

~

Enter self-seriousness, exit humor. Exit humor, exit sanity.

—WILLIAM KIRK KILPATRICK

With the fearful strain that is on me night and day, if I did not laugh I should die.

—ABRAHAM LINCOLN

Interlude:

A Positive

Mom...

A Positive
Mom…

~

…*Laughs Easily*

Kids won't remember a spotless house; they will always remember the times when you dropped everything to laugh with them. Just to keep my sense of humor and sanity, I used to pretend I was writing a column on the funny things kids do and say. (Tip: Write these things down right away!) Who would have dreamed that these scribbled notes from a harried mother would end up as the foundation for a writing and speaking career?

…*Blooms Where She's Budgeted*

When you have young kids and stay at home, the money is usually verrrry tight. This can be frustrating, sometimes even embarrassing. I drove an old STATION WAGON (back then, minivans were what the cool moms drove) for several years because it was cheap (as in "given to us") and held plenty of kids—along with their accompanying minnow buckets, fishing poles, assorted critters and wet bathing suits. Be creative—do picnics in the park instead of McDonald's, make your own play-dough, shop for resale bargains. Love, laughter, creativity, and your presence will make up for the shortage of almost any material goods.

...Tries to Find Some Way to Say "I Love You" Every Day

So you might forget to sign their homework papers. Perhaps you sent them to school with nonmatching shoes on their feet. Gave them Frosted Flakes for dinner last night. But if you found a way to tell them you love them, much will be forgiven. Three magic phrases guaranteed to bring a grin: "I sure do love you, kiddo." "You are my sunshine, did you know that? You bring so much joy to my heart." "I'm so proud of you! Way to go!"

...Relaxes with Her Flaws

Remember, the more you relax with your imperfections and theirs, the less chance you'll raise a little obsessive-compulsive perfectionist. Teach them by modeling that there are some things you don't do very well, but you've learned to ask for help—and this gives other people the wonderful chance to feel needed! For example, if you failed Housekeeping 101, trade housecleaning with a Martha Stewart-type mom while you offer to baby-sit her kids or make dinner or wallpaper her bathroom. God makes us all different for a reason: We need each other!

...Realizes Her Children Are Also Here to Teach Her

What mother hasn't secretly wished she could be the one who gets to crawl up in someone else's lap to be held and rocked and loved and soothed? Just as our children reach for our hands in the dark, so we moms—on our own individual dark days— can always revert to being children with God, our Father. In fact, Christ said that to enter His kingdom and all He has for us, there's no other way to approach Him but to run into His arms, with the trust of a small child. Children teach us so much about God's love, and we really can't experience this in any other way than by becoming a parent. G.K. Chesterton once said, "I've learned more about God from observing children in nursery school than from all the great theologians."

(My book, *Milk & Cookies to Make You Smile*—available on my Web site, www.beckyfreeman.com—was written to remind us to keep our childlike hearts alive.)

...Gathers a Circle of Support

Perhaps young motherhood is the time of life when we most need other friends, particularly other mothers with kids the ages of our children. You can find them at MOPS (Mothers of Preschoolers) groups at churches, Mom & Tot classes at the YMCA, you can find them collapsed in exhaustion on small tables at fast-food playgrounds...Put in the effort it takes to gather a group of three or four fun moms that meet on a weekly basis to share ideas, frustrations, prayers, and funny stories. You might, as a group, decide to trade baby-sitting nights one month, or bake double batches of freezable casseroles or goodies together while the kids play, or take the kids on a field trip to the zoo. Moms need moms to keep from feeling isolated and overwhelmed.

...Gives Her Kids a Hope-Filled Vision of the Future

Limit TV watching—particularly the evening news. In fact, many bright and decidedly sane people have chosen not to watch television news ever again. Period. Basically the news (and TV is the worst) is a collection of the most horrible happenings in the world, condensed and served up to American families daily, at six and ten. It is not realism—it is a formula for depression. It's no wonder our kids and teens are suffering from depression and apathy more than any other generation.

Our kids desperately need us to affirm a future filled with bright, purposeful, joy-filled lives. Assume that they will do well, and convey to them that God has created them to accomplish marvelous things. Have fun wondering and dreaming with them about what those things might be, as they toddle, walk, and eventually fly from our parenting nests.

A Funny Story

~

When my daughter was about four years old, I asked her what I thought was a very nonsexist question: "Rachel, would you rather be a doctor or a nurse?"

Thoughtfully, she finally replied, "I don't know. I guess I'll have to see which outfit looks best on me."

Wouldn't you know it, she's graduating from high school next year and is planning to become a professional makeup artist and beauty consultant!

CHAPTER 16

Love Me,
Love My Kids

~

We've all heard the saying, "The best way for a father to love his children is to love their mother." Well, I'm thinking about making a new cross-stitched saying: "The best way to love a friend is to love her children."

Some of my earliest memories are of playing in the yard of the student housing where we lived while my daddy was finishing his college degree. My mother and her girlfriends kept a lazy eye on us kids while they chatted and giggled in the sunshine. In cold weather, they often played cards while half-a-dozen or so of us played underneath the table and around their feet.

On hot summer days, the sound of the Popsicle Man driving by in his "Pop Goes the Weasel" truck created near panic among us. What if he went by before we could get permission and a nickel? Thankfully, our moms usually came through for us, and after the truck pulled away from the curb, I would sit on the front porch with my neighborhood buddies, licking the sticky grape coldness. I had a feeling of belonging and security just knowing I was a part of this happy community of women and children. When we would hear our mothers laugh out loud through the screen door from the kitchen, we knew that all was right in our sunlit world.

Time passed, and I grew up and married, but for an awkward while I was stuck in a no-man's-land of female friendship. I was just 17, too young to really feel a part of the upwardly mobile women in the Young Married Class at church. At the same time, since I was a married woman, I felt out of sync with other teenage girls. So in those in-between years, Mother and her friends often adopted me into their lunch group. I ate it all up—the food, the conversations, the gossip, and most of all, the laughter.

One of my favorites from among my mother's friends is Almedia—dear, precious Almedia. She knows the best books to read, finds the perfect cards to give, searches out the hottest bargains in town, and owns a deep but lilting Louisiana laugh. I've watched her and Mother through the years, laughing their way through seasons of serenity and seasons of crisis, and I've learned the critical therapeutic value of a Good Lunch Buddy.

When *Worms in My Tea* first came out, I arrived home one afternoon to find the following message on my recorder from Almedia. (I copied it down because it was my very first "fan" message and I was afraid I might not get another one.)

"Becky," the voice said, "I just finished reading your and your mother's darling book, and I'm just so full. Full of laughter and tears all at the same time. I always knew you were special and would do special things."

When she heard mother and me on a radio interview in her city, she drove up to the studio—while the live show was in progress—and tapped on the window. After we were off the air, she handed me a set of earrings she had just found at a boutique around the corner. "They were calling to me," she laughed. "They were saying, 'Buy us for Becky!'" And then, like the good fairy, she was gone.

Mother's close friends seem to have very naturally loved me and my brother and sister, and they continue to inquire regularly as to how we're getting along. I feel that my best friends' children are partially mine and vice-versa. The more adopted "aunties" in the world, the healthier our nation's kids. (Hey, there's another saying to cross-stitch!)

I learned a lot about adult female friendship from watching my mother with her friends. Maybe that's why I said yes to a crazy favor asked of me by my friend Shawn.

"Becky," her excited voice came over the phone, "do you know a preacher near you who could perform a wedding ceremony for me and Terry tomorrow? Maybe down by your lake?"

Shawn and I never had to tell each other who was on the other end of the line. Not after 17 years. "Hey, wait a minute!" I managed to get out in my surprise. "What about your big wedding plans?"

"We'll still go through with the church wedding as planned in a couple of months. But we want to be husband and wife NOW!"

Shawn, I thought, *are you sure about this?*

During the black months after her husband had left her on the grounds that "she had gained weight and he couldn't find a clean sock," Shawn had continued to be the epitome of those individuals who know how to make lemonade out of lemons, bloom where they are planted, and make the most out of the circumstances (and just about every other "thought for the day").

With Shawn's bubbly personality, it didn't take long for a good-hearted, handsome Christian man who loved children to scoop her up and ask her to marry him. Shawn hadn't known Terry all that long, but she was not an airhead, fun as she was, and as she talked, I began to feel reassured she had carefully considered this decision. The least I could do was share her joy. I brought my mind back to the question she had asked: "Do you know a preacher near you who could perform a wedding ceremony for me and Terry tomorrow?"

"Well," I said, thinking hard, "the man who does dishes for me when I cater meals said he used to be a preacher. Would he do?"

"Perfect," she said. "And you can sing something pretty, can't you?"

"Um...Shawn...You are kidding about this, aren't you?"

"Nope. See you tomorrow night."

To make a long story short, I convinced my ex-preacher–dishwasher friend to perform an outdoor wedding ceremony "to go." Mary and Gary, other friends of ours, happened to drop by for coffee, and as soon as hasty introductions were made, they provided "the audience." The vows were short but very sweet. As the breezes coming off the lake blew gently around the lovestruck couple, I sang "God, a Woman, and a Man."

After the ceremony, we all walked up the hill to our house. I had thrown together an angel food cake from a mix, slathered it with Cool Whip, and called it a wedding cake. I handed the new couple a knife to cut the cake, and posed them so Scott could take a snapshot. When they applied knife to cake, it reminded me of a kid stepping on an innertube. The cake compressed every time they tried to make an incision. And over and over again it kept springing back up. With each attempt Shawn lost more control over her giggles. The newlyweds couldn't, for the life of them, get the knife to penetrate their wedding cake. They finally gave up and tore pieces off with their bare hands.

That night when I sank into bed, exhausted but happy, it dawned on me that I had just pulled together a wedding in 24 hours. What we won't do for our friends!

My mother and her girlfriends taught me well.

Bear one another's burdens, and so fulfill the law of Christ.

—Galatians 6:2 NKJV

Why Women
Need Friends

~

Women respond to stress differently than men do. Fortunately, we also have a better way to fight it: each other. Friendships between women are special. They shape who we are and who we are yet to be. They soothe our tumultuous inner world, fill the emotional gaps in our marriage, and help us remember who we really are.

But they may do even more. Scientists now suspect that hanging out with our friends can actually counteract the kind of stomach-quivering stress most of us experience on a daily basis. For instance, a landmark UCLA study suggested that women respond to stress with a cascade of brain chemicals that cause us to make and maintain friendships with other women.

If friends can counter the stress that seems to swallow up so much of our lives these days, if they can keep us healthy and even add years to our life, why is it so hard to find time to be with them? That's a question that also troubles researcher Ruthellen Josselson, PhD, coauthor of *Best Friends: The Pleasures and Perils of Girls' and Women's Friendships.* "Every time we get overly busy with work and family, the first thing we do is let go of friendships with other women," explains Dr. Josselson. "We push them right to the back burner. That's really a mistake, because women are such a source of strength to each other. We nurture one another.

"And we need to have unpressured space in which we can do the special kind of talk that women do when they're with other women. It's a very healing experience."

CHAPTER 17

Should We Hatch Young— Or Fly South for the Winter?

~

I often wondered why our best "couple" friends, Dean and Heather, continued to invite us over. Their peaceful home was uninhabited by small children, and their lifestyle was one of freedom and serenity. For six years I waddled into their immaculate home, eternally pregnant and holding at least one toddler or rambunctious child by the hand. Each of those years, they had definitely decided not to have children, and that was semi-final.

Yet, Heather seemed genuinely intrigued with us. She always plied me with questions like a reporter gathering information from some just-discovered aboriginal tribe. She seemed to find it absolutely fascinating that I could survive a life of four small children amid total disarray and still smile occasionally—even frequently.

Dean and Heather were the perfect modern host and hostess, cooking our scrumptious meals side by side and serving them together. But once our brood dropped off to sleep, Scott and I reveled in the soft music drifting from the stereo in the background, and in the uninterrupted and oh-so-adult conversation. Strangely, it often drifted to the Big Question—"What's a good reason and when is a good time, if ever, to have a baby?"

I'll have to admit, it wasn't easy to come up with a quick answer. And how could I risk ruffling such neatly placed feathers? Dean has a teenage son by a previous marriage whom he adores, and his father-instincts seemed to have been completely satisfied. Heather had a great job with an airline, and they frequently jetted off to New York or California or sometimes even Europe as nonchalantly as other young couples go out for dinner and a movie. Both were pursuing higher degrees.

Dean and Heather reminded me in many ways of my sister, Rachel, and her husband, Gilley. When they decided to have a child, they approached it with their usual careful deliberation and profound common sense. Their hesitation may have been related to the fact that Rachel had been present at the home birth of our third child—the one when the midwife didn't get there in time. Or it may have had something to do with the time she visited our little family (six in number by then) just after we moved into our 865-square-foot lake cabin. I think she may have been looking for reassurance when she wrote Mother and asked her if, in her opinion, having children in today's world was really a smart idea. This was Mother's reply:

Dearest Rachel and Scott [Gilley],

I can understand the logic of choosing not to have children in today's world. It's an awesome responsibility—to bring a person into being who will be a part of our lives as long as we live, and sometimes that means an unending responsibility. Children can bring us a good deal of pain, some more than others. But they can also bring unmatched joy. What more worthwhile and adventurous thing could we do with our lives than to shape and mold another human being? It's certainly true that life can be so much more orderly and under control when only adults are involved. Once you children were raised, Daddy and I settled quickly into our comfortable, clean, quiet, unencumbered life. But—I wonder if we would enjoy it as much if we had always had it. Bearing and raising children is a sustained, intense course in learning to give—of every part of our being and life. Contrary to what you may be hearing today, I've found that the less centered we are on our selves, the happier our lives seem to be.

It is for certain that the intensity of love we feel for our offspring is unique, more gripping than any other emotion we experience, I think. But what if we should lose a child to an accident or an illness? The agony would be indescribable. Why not avoid the potential for pain? But the same thing is true, perhaps in lesser degree, about any one we love, and not many of us are willing to live life without love in order to avoid being hurt.

I'm afraid that people who make the decision not to have children when they're young have no idea what it will be like to be middle-aged and, finally, old. When your Nonnie was widowed and began to age at about 65, her children became her whole world, her emotional support, and often her providers. Then, when she became helpless, I shudder to think what would have been her lot at the nursing home if I had not been there most every day to check on her. I've seen the loneliness and desolation of the elderly who have no one to look after them. Maybe this isn't a good reason to bring a child into the world, but it certainly is a fringe benefit.

On the other hand, it may be that this is not a good time in history to bring children into the world. Who knows the future? It is certainly something to consider at any time, I suppose, and only the couple involved can make the decision. Just getting out of bed in the morning takes a lot of faith these days, but it is an adventure.

In case you and Gilley may be considering the option of not having children, Daddy and I want you to know it will be fine with us. We will not think less of you at all, but will certainly respect your judgment. And we will enjoy the times as four adults that we can share with you, times we can't really have with Becky and Scott for a few years yet. Their lives are different, and we enjoy different things with them. And you and Becky are so very different. I have loved sharing your very different lives and activities.

I'm intensely grateful to have had the precious children we had and to have been financially able to be at home with you as you grew up. I realize more every day how much harder it is for this generation to choose that lifestyle. I think if I knew for certain I would have to work all the time I was raising children, I might give it more serious thought before embarking on the adventure.

I will add this one last thought, and then close. Having children is like eating regular meals—wonderfully satisfying, but oh-so-daily. On the other hand, having grandchildren is like having a hot-fudge sundae when you haven't had sugar for a week! It's one of life's nicest surprises, one I didn't give much thought to until it happened to me. I can't imagine having missed it!

Bushels of love,
Mom

Within a year Mother was called to Virginia to look after her new grandson, Trevor, and two years later, we got this letter from my sister:

> I'm tired! But mostly we are enjoying Trevor so much. He's so sweet and bright and just loves a good time (and we wondered why he didn't want to sleep when he was newborn!). BRIGHT EYES has remained true to his birth nature. What a tremendous blessing he is. If (God forbid) he were gone tomorrow, I would still feel tremendously blessed to have known him. That's not meant to be morbid—just a statement of gratitude that God has entrusted him to us at all.

∼

Now I guess you're wondering about our yuppie friends Dean and Heather. Dean is 40 now. His hair is thinning just a tad and turning a distinguished shade of gray. Our friendship has only grown deeper over the years. Scott often speaks of Dean's ability to make others feel completely loved and accepted.

When Dean completed his doctoral program this winter, we celebrated with them over pizza and Cokes. Heather is just finishing her master's degree. Lest you think they have become all work and no play, they've also invited us to share a luxury condo in Florida on two separate occasions, and we are looking forward to doing it again this summer. It's great to have friends who are footloose and fancy-free.

Well—sort of. I should also mention that joining us last year on the Florida vacation was their tiny one-year-old daughter, Nicole, who has the biggest bluest eyes I've ever seen. And did I tell you about sharing her parent's excitement as they watched her first reaction to the waves and salt and sand? Or about how

Dean carries her everywhere in his backpack while Heather soaks up every sweet new word Nicole says, with the delight only a mother of a toddler can experience?

Oh, yes—and I should also mention that Dean and Heather loved being parents so much that they decided to expand again. Their question, "What is one good reason to have a baby?" appeared to have changed dramatically after they'd experienced the reality of a child looking up at them from their arms. As I watched our two friends fall in love with their daughter, that haunting question seemed to have been replaced by an unspoken conclusion—"Give me my own sweet baby! Who needs a reason?" So this summer Nicole will be accompanied to Florida by her new baby brother.

It was important to Dean and Heather that their new son carry a special name—the name of someone they loved and admired—a good and loyal friend. On the day the new baby was born, Dean called to tell us the name they had chosen for their newborn son. He would be called—Scott. On hearing the good news, my husband's eyes shone with pleasure all day.

During their recent visit to our house, we watched Dean and Heather unpack diapers and baby food and strollers and playpens and pacifiers and baby wipes from their family car while Scott and I told them about the first-ever real vacation we are planning to enjoy alone together—jetting away for four days in Colorado. The irony was not lost on us at all, and the four of us smile and wonder at the reversals that have taken place in our lives. Funny, they didn't seem to envy us our trip.

I was relieved and pleased to see that Heather had happily discovered the secret of nesting mothers the world over: Sure—kids can be a real pain. But during our visit, as Heather sat rocking baby Scott while Nicole laughed and played with my children nearby, Heather smiled and her voice grew tender.

"Becky, thanks for encouraging me to do this. I'm so glad I didn't miss getting to be a mother."

As I said, there are some things in life—like watching a jet-setting, career-oriented friend turn into mother-hen mush—you just have to experience for yourself.

Behold, children are a gift of the LORD,
the fruit of the womb is a reward.

—PSALM 127:3 NASB

CHAPTER 18

Lizards in
My Living Room

~

As we've said, my mother grew up dirt poor in an old house with dusty wood floors, a house where no one ever knew which room or bed or brother or sister they'd end up sleeping in or with at the end of a long day. Imagine her delight when she married my father, who took her away from all that to a brand-new home in the suburbs, complete with built-in appliances, a fireplace, plush carpet, two bathrooms, and separate bedrooms for each child.

Imagine her shock when my husband and I moved our four children to the country into a small cabin with dusty wood floors, a house where no one ever knew which room or bed or brother or sister they'd end up sleeping in or with at the end of a long day. Clearly, there is a vast difference between the housing preferences and lifestyles my mother and I have chosen, whether out of choice or necessity, I'm not always altogether sure. At least Scott and I are surrounded by leafy timber and sparkling water, but anyway you look at it, we seem to have created our own private demographical niche. We like to think of ourselves as Baby Boomers in the Boonies.

From the time I was a young girl, I dreamed of living in a cottage, complete with picket fence, nestled somewhere in

.ock's forest. It would be right out of the pages of a story-
.. I've since learned there is more to living near the edge of
forest than encountering an adorable family of talking
ars and bowls of steaming hot porridge. And some of the
ntruders who have shown up in our backyard have very little
in common with an innocent little girl wearing satin ribbons in
her boing-yoing curls.

Neither did I imagine that the cottages I had loved in childhood fairy tales did not come equipped with dishwashers,
garbage disposals, and central heat and air. The picket fence
didn't materialize, either. I soon learned that picket fences do
not good neighbors make in this laid-back lakeshore community. But some days, actually, I have felt I could use a fence
something on the order of the ones they used in *Jurassic Park*—
like the day Gabe came running into the house, his eyes bug-
ging out.

"Mom!" he shouted, "There are cows in our backyard! And
they've got humongous things sticking out of their heads."

Right. Of course. Children do have such creative imagina-
tions, don't they? However, at Gabe's insistence, I decided to
humor him by following his skipping, pointing figure outside
to see whatever he had imagined. And there they were—a nice
little herd of Texas longhorns, grazing happily in my backyard.
Gabe and I stood in the doorway and watched them for about
ten minutes, and eventually they lumbered off into the woods,
never to be seen again.

The longhorn cattle were probably the largest animals we
have entertained (so far), but there have been any number of
other interesting visitors from the nearby enchanted woods.
For several weeks, a furry family of baby possums occupied our
laundry room. Among their other activities, they enjoyed a
delightful game of peek-a-boo with my husband as he ironed
his shirt in the mornings. (I could say that I was ironing his
shirt, but then this story really would be a fairy tale.) Like so

many species, possums are actually quite cute until they get to be teenagers. During their rocky adolescence they sprout needle-sharp teeth, stay out all night having wild parties, and deposit revolting possum pellets in clothes hampers full of freshly folded laundry. And if you think a cat has nine lives—wait until you try to say "adios" to a possum. Take our advice and forget it. They are immortal.

Because of the wildlife-refuge atmosphere of our home, it causes us major concern when city dwellers come to stay with us overnight. Take the time my father came out for a visit while Mother was away visiting Nonnie. This was back when our house was basically a large one-room cabin, Abe Lincoln style. Daddy slept on the foldout couch maybe 15 feet away from where Scott and I snoozed in our double bed, which barely fit into the opposite corner of the room.

At about 2 A.M., Gabe's pet anole (a green chameleon-type lizard) decided to explore my forehead. Even in the world in which I live, I was taken by surprise, to put it mildly. I sat bolt upright and screamed, waking Scott and Daddy and all creatures great and small as far away as the other side of the lake. Once Scott got through to me and I realized the intruder was harmless, I fell back onto my pillow with a thud and into the soundest stages of deep sleep. Daddy, however, stayed stuck until morning in a wide-awake version of the well-known REM (Rapid Eye Movement) stage.

So. Why did we move to a cabin in the woods instead of living in a condo overlooking a golf course? I'll be honest. It was partly preference, and partly financial necessity. We wanted to raise our children in the country, preferably on a lake, and this cabin was what we could afford. As God provided us with a little money here and there we were able to add on, inch by inch. And we never looked back once we made the decision to live here. Even when the sewer backed up and the toothed critters threw nocturnal parties, Scott and I declared this to be

e, Sweet Home." This piece of ground is where our roots
nking. It's where I want to watch my grandchildren fish
swim, and teach them to say "great blue heron."

Like the pioneer man and woman of *Little House* days,
cott and I took joint pride in building a homestead, plank by
plank. Of course, I'm speaking figuratively about my actual
involvement in the homebuilding projects. Most of my heavy
efforts involved asking, "Ya'll want some iced tea?"

Scott's family, especially his dad, put in many hours of
barn-raisin' on our behalf. My folks contributed elbow grease,
paint, curtains, and decorative touches. Both sets of our parents
made generous financial donations to the cause on special
occasions—pure gifts of love. Even Zach and Zeke hammered
on the construction of what became their upstairs loft. It was
quite the extended family affair.

∾

Still, my mother sometimes worried, as all mothers do,
about my happiness and contentment level. One time at a
book-signing, we had a few minutes' gap between throngs of
customers, which gave us a chance to chat. We had time to
cover the theological foundations of American history and how
many angels we supposed could fit on the head of a pin, and
then we went on to the more mundane events of life—like
longhorn cattle in the flower garden and possum fangs in the
laundry room. Finally Mom asked me a question I think may
have been on her mind for some time.

"Becky, do you feel like you've had a hard life?"

I knew she was comparing my life to hers when she had
been my age. We had talked about this in a general way
before—that as my generation settled into adulthood, our lives

were very different from the lives of her generation at the same stage.

"I think," Mother had often said, "that my generation was privileged to live for a few brief years in a golden blip in time. A college degree in the '50s almost automatically meant a stable job in a stable company, a nice home, a new car. It wasn't that hard to have 'the good life.'"

On the other hand, my generation, the Baby Boomers, did not find the steps to the good life as easy to climb. College degrees in some fields are often a dime a dozen. As a result we tend to overextend our credit cards to live up to the image of the settled adults we remember from childhood. But things are not the same for us. They simply are not.

My friend—and insightful author—Paula Rinehart wrote a book that helped Mother and me both understand the dreams dreamed and the disappointments faced by my generation. It is aptly titled *The Cleavers Don't Live Here Anymore*. In comparing Mother's Post-war Generation to my crowded Boom Generation, Paula writes, "The fine irony is that our experience is practically the reverse of our parents'. The hardest years of their lives were, for the most part, their early years—the proving ground from which they moved on to better things."

For much of my generation, the reality is that we have already lived out the most prosperous portion of our lives— and it happened to have taken place in our childhood. The adult portion of our lives is proving to be the most economically difficult for many of us. And because we had such high expectations of success, our generation has had to deal with a few unpleasant realities—for instance, that we can't have everything we want when we want it without getting in so deep over our heads that we will possibly never see daylight again.

Mother's generation had been thoroughly warned about debt by frugal parents who drummed into them the importance of living within one's income. Once television commercials and easy credit permeated the very air they breathed, many of them often forgot the ancient wisdom, and many of their children were never told it.

Ah, well. So how did I answer Mother's question "Do you feel like you've had a hard life?" Actually, the answer came easily.

"No, I really don't." I paused and reflected. "Sure, there have been struggles and disappointments and even jealousy at times over what you and Daddy were able to have—and on one income. But somewhere fairly early along our way, I gave up the comparisons.

"Instead, I found myself reading stories of people in India and other poverty-stricken countries. I read the true story of Corrie ten Boom's life in a Nazi concentration camp. Alongside these people's life experiences, I felt spoiled and rich just remembering that I had a roof over my head, food to eat, and a family that loved me."

Mother was smiling, and her eyes reflected something wonderful to me. Was it respect—maybe even pride in what I was saying?

"For me," I went on, "It boils down to this. I can compare myself to The Lifestyles of the Rich and Famous or The Starving in Africa. One encourages discontent, the other immense gratitude. I'd lots rather spend my days with a thankful heart."

Not long after that day, I received a card in the mail. It had a picture of a horse that had apparently leapt over a fence and landed smack on its head. In the caption the horse says, "Oh, look! A four-leaf clover!" Inside, Mother had scribbled, "Couldn't help sending this—it reminds me so much of you."

One question I hear fairly often from the audiences I speak to is, "How do you cope with the irritations in your life—how can you laugh at what other people see as humiliating disasters?"

I often answer with the eloquence of a seasoned philosopher, "I have really low standards."

But seriously, I honestly wouldn't trade my lifestyle for the one my mother chose and was able to afford at my age. I would encourage every grown daughter—listen to your inner voice, that voice in your heart that whispers, "Go here, young woman"—wherever that may be. Even if it is a very different place from what your mother may have imagined for you. Ultimately, our happiness is all that mothers really want. So follow YOUR unique rainbow, and don't worry, be happy.

For me, crazy country living, somehow, has always seemed RIGHT—it's where I belong and I feel "I'm home" as I sit on the porch swing—even with (or perhaps, ESPECIALLY with) the lizards, possums, and longhorns that drop by for visits.

Brothers, whatever is…excellent or praiseworthy—
think about such things…For I have learned to be
content whatever the circumstances. I know what it is
to be in need, and I know what it is to have plenty.
I have learned the secret of being content
in any and every situation.

—PHILIPPIANS 4:8,11-12

Follow Your Star

~

Author Martha Beck calls it "finding your North Star"—finding that unique life you were meant to live. Sometimes it lines up with Mom's imagined North Star for you, and sometimes it doesn't. You have to find the courage to lovingly say, "Mother, I love you. But I'm reaching for the stars God put in my own heart."

When you're following a direct course to your North Star, you'll inevitably make decisions that should, by the social self's reckoning, be scary and depressing. You may be surprised when you don't feel the fear or sadness that seems warranted by the situation. Instead, you'll bounce around like Ebenezer Scrooge after the ghosts finished with him: smiling at strangers, finding infinite patience for children and the mentally ill, slowing down traffic to let cats and turtles make their way across the street. Bitter, unhappy people will want to slap you, but you'll love them anyway.

This maddeningly good mood often comes over people who have found a part of their true path.

CHAPTER 19

My Daughter, the Stealth Toddler

~

I remember well the day I dared to pray for a daughter. I managed to get my two rambunctious boys down for a nap, then plopped myself upon the couch in the living room and faced the questions I asked myself every afternoon at this time: Should I join the boys in Slumberland, have my "quiet time," or run through the house like a mad woman and try to straighten it up?

But just then I noticed my hope chest in the corner of the room. It had been a present to me from Scott on my sixteenth birthday. I decided to skip the nap, the quiet time, and the housecleaning, and I chose instead to take a walk down Memory Lane. Soon I found myself sorting through stacks of memorabilia while breathing in the pungent scent of cedar, when suddenly I came across—it. I had forgotten about this delicate baby dress I had been given so long ago, and I realized that, along with the dress, I had also laid aside a dream. Now the hidden desire of my heart washed over me once again.

The story that goes with this tiny dress may be hard to believe. Before I go on, it is important that you keep in mind that Scott and I were possibly the most serious-minded and lovesick teenagers to ever grace this fair planet.

The summer we fell in love we happened to be on a short-term mission trip to Central America. In Guatemala, Scott and I visited the local market one afternoon. At one booth, we stopped to watch the skillful native women as they hand-stitched exquisite designs on articles of clothing with brilliantly colored thread. A tiny, simple dress caught my eye. It was obviously made for a baby girl—its gauzy white cotton embroidered and fringed in a gentle blue. I looked at the adorable dress, then at Scott. He looked back at me, and before I realized what was happening he had bought the dress and given it to me.

"Someday," he said softly, "this will look awfully cute on our little girl."

Mind you, Scott and I were 15 and 16 and hadn't even shared our first kiss yet, and there we were daydreaming about having a family. Wouldn't my parents have DIED?

Sitting there on the floor beside the cedar chest that afternoon, with our two sons sleeping in the next room, I fingered the delicate fabric of the Guatemalan baby dress. It was a reminder of an old dream, tucked underneath a scrapbook labeled "All My Boyfriends." (I had started the scrapbook at age 14, not realizing it would be all of two paragraphs long when I met my One and Only True Love.) A rush of emotion swept over me, and I began pouring my secret longings before the Lord.

"Dear Lord, you know how much I love my two boys. But this dress is so sweet and feminine! And I know Scott would kill me if I put it on Zach or Zeke. Even though I am strictly a female Female, I've managed to learn to mother two males made of frogs and snails and puppy-dog tails. I can now hold amphibians without dropping them in disgust. I can make motorcycle noises and even play 'rassle.' But—there's a part of me that longs to braid hair with pink ribbons and play dress-up and have tea parties— with a child made mostly of sugar and spice. Maybe a little girl

who is a miniature version of myself? She'll probably be dark-haired and outgoing, round and short—and of course she'll most likely talk the ears off a mule, just like her mother.
"Oh, Lord—could I possibly have a daughter?"

～

The Lord made me wait all of ten months, and I must say, my little Answer to Prayer certainly made a grand entrance into the world. For starters, she didn't wait for the midwife, so her daddy "mid-husbanded" her into my waiting arms—a foreshadowing of things to come. As if by rote, Scott immediately announced our new baby was a boy. After all, he was familiar by now with such an announcement. Imagine our surprise when we discovered a few moments later that Scott had been quite mistaken in all the excitement—and we had been gifted with a gen-u-ine GIRL! A few weeks later I took the little embroidered dress from my hope chest, slipped it onto my little doll baby, and gazed in wonder at my dream come true. Well, almost...

Perhaps when the Lord formed Rachel Praise He wanted to show me that each child is His own unique creation. Or perhaps He knew that Scott couldn't handle more than one talkative brunette in this family. Whatever His reasoning, Rachel came to us with wisps of soft blonde hair and an amazingly quiet spirit. Now, I'm not talking about the regular type of "quiet," I'm talking about a semicomatose brand of "quiet." From the time our little girl was old enough to be aware of people, she developed the skill of "playing possum." Whenever someone would come over to coo over her and admire her, she'd focus straight ahead—her eyes looking completely vacant—and her body would turn to stone.

The frustrating part of all this was, when Rachel was alone with me and her brothers she would transform herself before our very eyes into an animated, gurgling baby. This pattern continued until she was three-and-a-half years old. She could talk my ears off as soon as a room was adult-free but stopped immediately when anyone wandered back into her "space"— like a game of freeze-tag! With adults other than myself and her grandmothers, she managed to communicate by shaking her head up and down or back and forth, hoping they could understand through her brown eyes what she was inexplicably afraid to say with her mouth. It appeared to all the world— with the exception of the aforementioned privileged few—that Rachel was hearing-impaired. I couldn't believe it. How could any child of mine not want to be the life of the party?

There were some benefits to Rachel's quiet nature. For one, she was extremely affectionate—and portable. I could take her to any meeting and be assured she would never utter a peep.

Though Rachel had turned out to be the silent type, do not think for a moment that this meant she was clingy and afraid of adventure. When she was just a few months old, we moved to our first place in the country, our nearest neighbors being a field away. Their two teenage daughters, Tracy and Dixie, loved to put Rachel in an open grain pail and carry her around in it when they went to feed their huge Charolais heifer, B.J.

When my baby girl reached the crawling age she often wore what I called "Sweet Pea" nightgowns. Zach and Zeke loved nothing more than to step on the long hem of her sleeper, keeping her from actually covering any ground. She quickly learned to deliver the ear-splitting squeal all brothers love to hear. They also taught her to stick out her tongue on command, the signal being "Be a sassy girl, Rachel!" How ironic. She had the gall to stick out her tongue at strangers, but she couldn't bring herself to say the standard "bye-bye" or "patty-cake" in front of an audience to save her life.

We soon learned that, though our little daughter was the silent type, she was faster than greased lightning. She had hurried herself into the world well before the arrival of the midwife and had pretty much kept right on going. Because she was a fast little bugger and a remarkable climber, her quietness was actually dangerous at times.

One cold spring morning when Rachel was about 18 months old, she and I had enjoyed a bath together. I had wrapped her in a towel and begun to fluff her dry, but before I knew what had happened, she popped out of the towel like a banana out of its peel and shot out the bathroom door. I grabbed an old robe, donned it on my dripping torso, and ran after her in hot pursuit. By the time I reached the living room, the open front door told the tale.

I ran outside without my shoes, wet and freezing, and began to search the country landscape. As I tripped over rocks and crawled under barbed wire, I called out for my escaped toddler, who was adorned this cold morning with nothing but her birthday suit. She was nowhere to be seen. My first thought was of Tracie and Dixie carting Rachel around their huge heifer's pen, and I felt a surge of anxiety. Surely not!

I raced to B.J.'s pen. No Rachel. I looked across the pasture and remembered the other, even larger, Black Angus bull—and real fear gripped me! As I ran through a field of stickers in my bare feet, I tripped and felt my big toe snap. Shaking off the pain and the blood, I bolted toward the bull and found him contentedly chewing his cud, alone in the pasture. No sign of a naked baby, whole or flat.

Drained and near panic, I raced towards Dixie and Tracy's house to see if their parents might be home so they could join me in the search for my pint-sized streaker. When I reached their back porch, breathless and bruised, I was going so fast I nearly tripped over a bare-skinned and sassy little toddler sitting on the steps. There was Rachel in all her glory, her tongue sticking straight out in my direction. I decided at that moment she definitely takes after my mother!

As Rachel passed from two to three-going-on-four, she began to especially adore her daddy, and the feeling was completely mutual. We knew this, not because she told him so or ever actually spoke, but because she freely offered hugs, kisses, and lap-holding privileges to him.

During Scott's nightly routine of rocking her to sleep, they spoke not a word, but were completely content with their silent cuddling ritual. Eventually, however, Scott began to long to hear the sound of his daughter's voice directed at him. For several weeks we tried everything we could think of without success, until finally the day came when we experienced the Big Breakthrough.

On this particular evening, Scott gathered up Rachel in his arms along with her favorite storybook and retired with her to the couch in the living room, where they could be alone. His plan was to read her the book and purposely mispronounce and leave out some words. We knew how Rachel hated to leave any wrong unrighted. (She still hates it!) Scott told us later what had transpired.

"Well, it was pretty slick. I started to read and I left out some words here and mixed up others there. Rachel was in agony, shaking her head 'no' so hard that her short blonde hair was flying. I just kept right on reading. Pretty soon she put her face directly in front of mine and shook her head back and forth until I thought it might spin off her little neck. Finally, she could take it no more.

"'Daddy!' she blurted out, 'It not Berry the Moose, it Vera the Mouse!'"

Scott paused thoughtfully, then continued with a grin: "She proved me wrong, but those were the sweetest words I ever heard."

... Those who could not speak will shout and sing!
—Isaiah 35:6 tlb

CHAPTER 20

Motherhood Means Never Having to Say, "I'm Organized"

~

Readers of our book *Worms in My Tea* will not be surprised to find out that my sister, Rachel, majored in office management during college. In that book, I gave an example of what it was like for me, the Right-Brain Creative Type, to have a sister who was clearly a Left-Brain Organizer Type.

I wrote, "When we were children living at home, her belongings were so organized that I could not filch so much as one M&M from a mammoth Easter basket without being called to account for it." I don't know how she knew, but she always knew.

When Rachel moved back in with the folks after two years of being on her own, things generally went very well. She was determined to preserve her new independence and felt she was becoming more and more her own person. This was a great consolation until she realized just how independent the folks had become. She had imagined them pining away after she, their last child, had left home, and she was somewhat shaken to see how well they had adjusted to an empty nest.

"Boy," she told me over the phone from Virginia, "it kind of hurt my feelings when I had to take Mom's face in my hands and say, 'Remember me? I'm Rachel—your daughter.'"

Eventually Rachel got a job in Virginia and settled in there, getting her own apartment with a couple of great roommates. At this point, she felt she could relax. She was definitely her own person in her new surroundings, and she felt delightfully independent. Then she was invited to a wedding shower, a wedding shower to which Mother was also invited. She chose her own gift, bought her own wrapping paper and ribbon, and got her own card, even though they both knew the bride and could have shared a gift. When she arrived at the party, she placed her gift in a huge pile of other gifts.

"There were probably a hundred gifts in that pile," she told me later on the phone, "and only two of them were wrapped in identical wrapping paper. Guess whose they were?" I could tell by the tone of her voice that this was not what she had expected.

"Don't tell me. One was Mother's—and the other belonged to my independent, one-of-a-kind little sister, perhaps?"

"Mom thought it was a hoot, of course," Rachel deadpanned.

"I have warned you about the Omnipresent Mother Syndrome, haven't I? Mother even said that she hears Nonnie whispering advice in her ear. It's comforting to know you're also experiencing this. Give it a few years, and mark my words—you, I, and mother will be virtual triplets."

~

In *Worms in My Tea* I described the home births of my four children, which all took place during the Mother-Earth, Back-to-Nature era. To say I had been naive about the anesthetic effectiveness of proper breathing and good coaching during childbirth would be understatement at its grossest. I had been told that labor was merely hard work. Well, I know hard work when I see it. Labor was PAIN. "As memories of my totally natural Lamaze, Leboyer, LaLudicrous births swept over me, all I could think was, *What was I thinking?"*

On the other hand, Rachel "went into labor after a full night's rest at about seven in the morning on her day off. Seven and a half hours later, she called me from the exquisitely beautiful and home-like birthing room at the hospital to tell me in graphic detail of the two painful contractions she had endured before calling for the epidural."

As you would expect of this couple, they had spent long hours planning how they could manage to birth this new baby and rear him without losing control or making mistakes. First and foremost in their plan was for the father to spend adequate time with his child, starting from the moment they took the baby home. So how did Rachel's serene and ordered life survive the introduction of a child?

The first thing that shattered the composure of my sister and her husband, Gilley, was that Trevor cried. They found that he cried even when he couldn't possibly be hungry and when his diaper was toasty dry. Rachel, Gilley, and Mother spelled each other walking the floor at night for the first week or so, and the young couple's anguish knew no bounds. The new father could not find time to go to work, what with all his new responsibilities at home, but when he called his boss to tell her so, there followed an interesting conversation.

"Ann," he told his boss, "I don't know when I'll be able to get back to work. The doctor has diagnosed our baby as having colic." The boss, being female and a mother of lengthy tenure, suppressed a smile.

"Gilley," she said, trying not to laugh, "the baby will be okay without you, but I may not. I'll see you tomorrow in the office, okay?"

Are you beginning to get the picture? I had also written of baby Trevor, "I fully expect that my new nephew will...develop into a child prodigy at the piano, and as a teenager frequently ask, 'What else can I do to help you, Mother?'" After Trevor had turned two-and-a-half, I had a telephone conversation with his mother, and I decided I might have been prematurely and overly envious.

"I've got to find a way to get organized," Rachel said, and there was a ragged edge to her voice. "Working 20 hours a week shouldn't be that big a deal, should it? I feel like I'm losing control. Not long ago I had Trevor in the bathtub and the phone rang. I debated not answering it but I was expecting an important call. I was close enough where I could hear him splashing and talking happily to himself, so I knew he was all right. Even so it took longer than I expected, and when I started back up the hall toward the bathroom, I could see water gently billowing onto the carpet.

"Just as I rounded the bend and threw on my brakes, Trevor was emptying the last toy bucket full of water out of the tub. THEN the doorbell rang. It was the designer-suited single gentleman from downstairs, saying there was water leaking through the light fixture of his garage and onto his $30,000 Mercedes, and asking if I knew anything about it. I thought only a few seconds before I told him what I knew on the guy who had done it, and I promised our neighbor I'd see it didn't happen again.

"Fortunately we have a good friend who is an electrician, and we were able to prevail upon him to fix the fixture, but then last week I was rushing to get things together so I could get in to work. I had turned on the faucet in the bathroom to let the water warm up, and then I heard Trevor in the refrigerator in the kitchen. He's still in that 'take the lid off and pour stuff on the floor' stage, so I had to tend to him—and by the time I got the juice poured and his bib on and had him sitting at his feeding table, I remembered that I'd left the water running in the bathroom.

"I took off down the hallway just in time to see the familiar water doing its familiar billowing toward the hall. I checked my watch to see how late I was going to be to work and wondered if I could get out of the condo before Mr. Picky-About-His-Fancy-Car appeared at the door again. I told Scott that if he did, he was not to hesitate—tell him our two-year-old had done it!"

And the waters prevailed exceedingly upon the earth...

—GENESIS 7:19 KJV

CHAPTER 21

Kitchen-Table Confessions

~

Oh, the news from my sister's house was delicious—absolutely delicious. And of course when Mother and I met for lunch the next week, we had a great time laughing about Trevor's antics and his parents' efforts to manage them.

"I wonder if they ever think of that letter you wrote telling them what a great idea it is to have kids?" I asked.

"I don't know," she grinned, "but I may stay out of Virginia for a year or two. Maybe by the time Trev is in first grade, I can ask forgiveness." Having finished lunch, she leaned back in her chair, and I got the feeling there was something on her mind.

"Speaking of forgiveness," she began, "I've been thinking a lot about forgiveness—how much it meant to me when your Grandaddy Jones let me know he regretted some of the bitter things that had passed between us. And I know I've made a lot of mistakes in raising my children. There are failures that I'm painfully aware of, but I expect there were failures in areas that were important to you that I don't even have a clue about. Is there anything in particular I need to ask your forgiveness for?"

"Well-l-l-l—" I thought for a minute, and said the first thing that came to my mind. "I sort of wish you and Daddy had been more open about your arguments. Not that I wish you had yelled at each other a lot or anything like that. But I'd like to have seen more conflict and clashing of opinions—like with those earthy, emotional families from romantic Mediterranean countries in the movies.

"Then I'd like to have observed the process of resolution. It might have helped me to not have been so shocked when I had my first blowup with Scott. I think I grew up believing I'd never have a real fight with my husband." When I looked up from my salad, Mother had a very peculiar expression on her face.

"That's very interesting," she said, "because when I asked your sister the same question, she said she wished I could have controlled my anger a little more carefully. She probably had something in mind like those proper and respectful families from English movies. Isn't it interesting how siblings can see the same parent so differently? Wonder what David would say."

I could imagine already what David would say and had to laugh. "Let me save you the trouble, Mom. David would have preferred you to be more laid-back and easygoing—a 'no problem' type. Then we could all have lived like the happy natives in South Pacific movies."

Mother looked more confused than ever. Could even a Supermom please every child? The more I thought about my own struggle to meet the individual needs of my four children, the more I empathized with my mother. I also felt a greater appreciation that she had tried so hard, and was trying even now, to do the impossible.

"Hey," I said gently, "forget Supermom. She's made out of plastic and paint, not flesh and blood."

"Thanks," she said, cupping her chin in her hand. "Actually, a little island vacation may sound pretty good by the time I finish this process. But you know what? You girls have surprised me. You didn't mention some of my failures that sometimes make me cringe when I just think of them. It never occurred to me that shielding you children from the disagreements your dad and I had might not be the best thing. I guess because there were so many storms swirling in my childhood home, I was determined to shield my own kids from that kind of thing.

"Just for the record, your dad and I have had some humdingers over the years—a few that were pretty serious. Does it help to know that?"

I nodded, somewhat relieved. Even so, I was pretty sure my and Scott's definition of a "humdinger" and Mother and Daddy's definition of it might not exactly coincide. But at least I knew there had been a few hitches in my parents' relationship over the years and, yes, it was reassuring.

Our coffee was lukewarm by now, so we signaled for a warm-up, and Mother continued. "I do apologize for ever trying to convey to you that Daddy and I have had a near-perfect marriage. You didn't see the behind-the-scenes work it took to arrive at this place of comfort and joy with each other. Believe me, darlin'—life is real and life is earnest. For everybody."

All have sinned and fall short of the glory of God...
There is now no condemnation for those
who are in Christ Jesus.
—Romans 3:23; 8:1

CHAPTER 22

A Legacy of Lovable Loonies

~

Our family reunions, in general, were always ripe with emotion (not to mention plenty of writing material). However, we wondered whether the Jones family would be the same after the matriarch, our beloved Nonnie, had passed on. I soon found that attending a Jones Family Reunion was still an Amazing Experience. Each time we gathered with Mother's side of the family and everybody reported on what they'd been up to, I always felt like asking, "Do other families do these kinds of things?" And a voice from deep inside would whisper, "I don't think so!"

As you might expect, this reunion was a crowded, noisy, lots-of-hugging, whoop-it-up, chocolate-covered affair. Aunt Etta flew in from Lubbock with no less than 12 chocolate-cream pies. A lesser woman would have concluded it couldn't be done, but not my Aunt Etta. She would bake the 12 pie shells and stack them one on top of the other in a hatbox that she carried onto the plane, the box swinging from one arm. Of course all this was accomplished with style, charm, and excellent posture. The gallon of chocolate-cream filling was divided into two plastic containers and stowed in a shopping bag that swung from her other arm. Whipped topping was purchased on arrival in Houston, and the orgy was on.

I always wondered what the other passengers on her plane might look like in the event of a severe turbulence or a rough landing. All I know is that my Aunt Etta would have been the picture of poise and grace—even with a faceful of pie filling.

On this occasion, Uncle J.R. was fresh back from Pennsylvania, where he had gone to appear as a contestant on Bill Cosby's quiz show, *You Bet Your Life.* Cosby chose him to match wits with the other contestants because Uncle J.R. was a bit unusual. At age 57, he was the Texas State Arm-Wrestling Champion, regularly defeating surprised young men in their 20s.

When our colossal dinner had settled, several of us left the table and headed for the kitchen to load our dessert plates with another round of Aunt Etta's chocolate pie. As we regathered at the table, my cousin Jamie—Uncle J.R.'s daughter—wandered in and joined us.

Now, I feel I must prepare you for Jamie. If any statement in this book stretches your capacity to believe, it will be this one: I'm not the only person in the world who can bring chaos out of order in no time at all. I have a counterpart in my cousin Jamie.

When people meet Jamie for the first time, they expect her to be, well…"together." For instance, when she started to tell us about her latest escapades, she looked like a gorgeous TV personality about to present a commentary on the latest world event. Big blue eyes danced with life in a beautifully tanned face. Frame the cherry-red mouth with dimples, the pretty face with cascading golden-blonde hair, and you begin to get the picture—newscaster, talk-show host, that sort of thing.

She folded her long, tapered hands over her crossed knees and started to tell us about her days as an aide in a California nursing home. How did this knockout blonde happen to be working as a nurse's aide in a place where the young usually don't hang out? Let's put it this way. In a Miss America Pageant, Jamie would have been chosen "Miss Compassionate."

"The hardest part about my job," she began, "was never having enough help. I had 12 patients to bathe and care for in an eight-hour period, so I never felt I was doing a really good job for any of them. They were precious to me, though, and I loved 'em, bless their hearts.

"One of my favorite patients was Spike, an ex–Aggie football player. He couldn't see, and he couldn't walk or talk, but he loved for any of the staff to ball up a pillow and throw it into his stomach like a football. He'd grab the pillow and hold it in the air like a football player who had just snagged an impossible pass. Then he'd duck his head, tuck the pillow under one arm, and bounce up and down in his wheelchair, mentally heading for the goal line. You could almost hear the roar of the crowd. I thought Spike was a ton of fun, and we played lots of football together. But I never heard Spike say a word.

"After I had been there a couple of weeks, the director sent me to his room with his usual oatmeal. 'Test it to make sure it's not too hot,' she warned. So I went to Spike's room and found him sitting in his wheelchair. If I hadn't had a breakfast tray in my hands I would have thrown him a pass to let him know I was there.

"'Hi, Spike,' I greeted him cheerily, 'how you doin'?' He grinned his toothless grin but made nary a sound. He had dropped his lap cover, so I found that for him and covered his feet and legs. Then I had to find myself a chair, and by the time I got situated I had forgotten all about the director's warning. Finally I scooped up a big bite of oatmeal and dumped it into Spike's eager mouth. I immediately learned that he could speak after all. He yelled at the top of his lungs, 'THAT'S HOT!'"

Jamie went on to tell us about her experience with the all-new electric beds in one of the nursing homes where she had worked as a temporary employee.

"At all of the other places I'd worked, we had to crank these beds by hand to elevate them. Since I'm tall, I was really tickled to discover that, by pushing a certain button, I could not only raise or lower the head of the bed, but make the whole bed slowly rise.

"So one evening I went in to get Mr. Shropshire ready for bed by helping him brush his teeth. He was lost in a reverie, his bedside radio softly playing music of the '40s in the dim evening light.

"Before I went into the bathroom to get his toothbrush, I punched the button to elevate his bed. In the bathroom I noticed someone had put one of his undershirts in the sink to soak, so I decided to rinse it out and hang it up to dry. Just about the time I got to the wringing-out part of my chore, I heard a loud scraping sound. I dropped the T-shirt and ran back into the room.

"I couldn't believe how high those electric beds would go! Mr. Shropshire was now even with my chest (remember, I'm tall), but that was not my biggest problem. Evidently the rail of the bed had caught the nightstand on the way up, and it was wedged between the bed and the wall. While I stood there, the radio slid off the stand and onto the bed, coming to a stop just under Mr. Shropshire's chin. It looked for all the world like Benny Goodman's band was broadcasting directly out of his chest. I didn't know whether to laugh or cry, but once I apologized, Mr. Shropshire didn't seem particularly upset."

We figured Mr. Shropshire probably thought he had been carried to the sky by the beautiful angel hovering over him.

"Here's one I almost forgot," she giggled. "Now guys, this happened while I was still in training, so it's understandable, okay?

"There was a Mr. Williams who needed help putting his false teeth in. He didn't particularly like to wear them and would have been more than happy just to gum it, but we always tried to make sure he had them in his mouth for meals. This particular morning I was in a hurry, so I whipped those dentures out and approached his wheelchair.

"'Come on, Mr. Williams, it's time for breakfast. I'm going to put your teeth in. Open wide.' He looked at me like he had no idea what I was talking about, so I opened his mouth for him, popped 'em in, and wheeled him into the dining room. I gave all the patients a tray and then observed them to make sure no one needed assistance. Just then I noticed that Mr. Williams was having trouble chewing his strawberries. This was odd, because he loved to eat, especially strawberries, and I had never noticed him having trouble chewing anything before.

"I walked over to investigate—and when he looked up at me, I was confronted by the strangest-looking set of dentures I had ever seen in my life. The top teeth were small and the bottom teeth were much bigger, giving Mr. Williams the appearance of a Pekinese dog. When it hit me that I had put the bottom plate on top and the top plate on the bottom, I started to laugh. I couldn't help it. I laughed 'til the tears ran down my face. I couldn't stop laughing, and I had to get someone else to put Mr. William's teeth in right so he could eat his breakfast."

Now I ask you—do other families do these kinds of things? I still don't think so!

While I and several of my cousins sat among the Older Generation of Joneses, telling our stories with the best of them, I recalled those reunions I had attended out in West Texas when I was a child. The kids had always played games on the living-room floor while the grown-ups had sat around the table after the meal telling tall and hilarious tales. Now, we were grown-ups, too. By Jove, we even got a little respect now and then!

When the party ended and the goodbyes could no longer be postponed, I watched each of my uncles take both Mother and Aunt Etta tenderly into their arms and kiss them, murmuring things like, "Bye-bye, sweetie," and "See you next time, sugar."

Aunts and cousins hugged and laughed like a gaggle of geese, each trying to outdo the others with their parting shots. Aunt Martha hugged me and warned, "Watch those kiddos, Becky. Don't let 'em sneak up on you and throw you in the lake, now!"

I settled into the car next to Mother, tired, happy, and ready to be home again. I had survived another Jones Family Reunion where we had laughed a lot, loved a lot, and eaten way too much once again. But still, it was a wonderful feeling. The "birds" in our family tree had rearranged themselves a bit, but the roots were still deep and strong, the trunk solid. And down among the lower branches, I thought I could almost make out the silhouette of a new nest. And—was that "Mr. and Mrs. Scott Freeman & Brood" written on the mailbox?

God sets the lonely in families.

—PSALM 68:6

CHAPTER 23

We're All Grown-Ups Here—Finally!

~

So far, this book has been pretty much a fun project, as we anticipated at the beginning. But now Mother and I come to the place where we need to make a confession. Although we have a great relationship, and as you can see from the stories we've shared, we enjoy each other tremendously, we would be a little devious if we didn't tell you some of the things we've worked through together. And we hope this may be the most encouraging part of the book, both to moms and daughters.

When my sister, Rachel, was in her early 30s, she was going through some intense and private inner struggling. She felt that part of her pain had to do with some of the ways my folks had dealt with her as she was growing up, particularly in the area of discipline. She wrote to David and me to ask if she was seeing this clearly. We replied yes, we agreed this had been a blind spot with our folks.

We all knew how much Mother, especially, wanted closeness in our family as we kids were now married adults with children. In order to give Mother this closeness—real closeness, not based on performance—Rachel felt that she needed to have a heart-to-heart talk with my parents about some of these old wounds. Since she was living in Virginia at the time and they were in Texas, she painstakingly crafted a very loving letter, and then called my parents and told them it was on the way:

"You've asked me, Mom, if there was something between us, and I've said no. But the truth is, there are some things I think we need to deal with."

Looking back on this now, I see what terrific courage it took for my sister to risk being honest. But at the time I was scared to death Mother might keel over in a dead faint, or fall into a bottomless pit of a deep depression, or worse. Generally, MY motto in life is "Let sleeping dogs lie!" "In other words, if it ain't broke past working, don't fix it!" As the consummate people-pleasing pacifist, I felt like crawling into a foxhole, putting both fingers in my ears, and waiting there until it was all over.

But—to my surprise and relief, a beautiful thing happened. The letter arrived in Texas. Within a few days, Daddy had the opportunity to be in Virginia on a business trip, which he extended in order to spend some time with Rachel. For three days—while Gilley baby-sat Trevor—Daddy and Rachel spent time in coffee shops and talked about the past over lunch. (Never underestimate coffee-shop therapy). Finally, on a deserted park bench by the ocean, they held each other and cried.

Rachel poured out her pain and felt free to specifically address the ways in which she had been hurt or disappointed by him at times. He was able to explain some of what his thinking as a parent had been and help her to understand in some areas. In other areas he could only say, "I'm so sorry, honey. If I had it to do over again, I wouldn't do it that way. Please forgive me."

By this point, there was no need to ask. And yes, I still think my father is an unusually wonderful man. But now we all know that nobody's perfect, not even my dad.

Then it was Mother's time to make the trip to Virginia. For the first couple of days, she and Rachel kept the conversation light as they shied away from The Subject. I learned later that Mom was actually anxious to discover what that strange barrier between them had been, and to remove it if at all possible.

The time they spent in coffee shops and over lunch was nice, but the barrier stayed right in place where it had been for a long time. Yet both were keenly aware of it. Then on the next-to-last day of Mother's visit, they pulled into the driveway after a visit to the grocery store, and the floodgates opened.

Womanlike, their tears started immediately, but there were never any harsh words. Rachel just explained how she had felt at times when she was a little girl, and Mother was able to say, "There was so much I didn't know, honey, as a parent"—and occasionally, "Here is what I was thinking, and here is why I handled it that way." Some of what Mother told her helped Rachel to see that, as the adult child of an alcoholic parent, Mother brought her own wounds and defenses into parenting.

Finally, while they held each other, Mother said through tears, "You are right about so many of those things. I was young, and I was selfish, too, at times. But—it was never because I didn't love you, honey! Please know, you were such a joy to us, even back then, and you've been so much fun to raise. And I am SO proud of you!"

And Rachel, bless her heart, sobbed out the healing words Mother also badly needed to hear. "I know, Mom. I love you, too. And I do forgive you."

∼

Finally, I knew the phone call had to be made. Mother answered on the third ring, and after a few words, I managed to say what I had called to say.

"Mother, since you've worked through some things with Rachel, you've asked me several times if there was anything we needed to talk about, and I've said no. But…there ARE some things, and I just don't think the two of us by ourselves can get through them. Would you consider working with a family counselor?"

"Of course!" she responded. "Let's do it!"

A friend of mine had recommended a counselor located in Dallas, between Mother's house in Bedford and my house in Greenville. At the time, Scott and I didn't have much money, but I explained to Mother that it was important to me to pay my half of the bill. I felt a therapist might help me put what I was feeling into words—much of it had to do with becoming "my own person" as all daughters have to do. I think God used even the pain of my pulling away from the desperate need of consistent, 100-percent approval from my mother in order to make both of us into healthier women, as well as make our relationship lots more real and even more fun.

Part of what I needed and wanted to come out of this was that Mom understand I was an independent and capable grown woman now. (Now that I am a mother of young adults myself, I do think it is tough for anyone who has seen you dribble carrots into a bib and helped you get your thumb unstuck from a Coke bottle to really see you as completely competent to handle life.) That settled, we came to the really BIG problem. How were the two of us independent, capable women going to manage to navigate the unfamiliar terrain of North Dallas, and particularly the frantic North Dallas Tollway?

We both did it, but when we met in the parking lot at the counselor's office, I couldn't help asking, "How many extra quarters did YOU have to pay before you got off at the right exit?"

"Three," she admitted, grinning. "What about you?"

"Two!" I announced triumphantly.

We had to make that harrowing trip about three times before the garbage and cobwebs that had accumulated in hidden places of our relationship were swept away. Some cobwebs had been there a long time, others were more recent. There had been misunderstandings on both sides, some of which evaporated once we could be honest and open with each other. On one particular day, the tears and words flowed in torrents from both of us, leading up to a scene that would have made any movie director proud. At the end of the storm, we fell into each other's arms, both crying, "I love you!" The counselor, a woman about my age, watched us with eyes as big as silver dollars, and with a grin that said, "I don't think I've ever seen a mother and daughter quite like you two."

To this day we both would still like an explanation of her remark, but at the time we were too exhausted to ask. Drained, but full of hope, we both felt that a new honesty and openness in our relationship had been established.

Interestingly, Mother later told both Rachel and me that this was one of the hardest but most helpful times of her life, and she thanked us for it. "I marvel," she said, "that the two of you loved me enough to open your hearts and to risk hearing my heart as well. To be honest, it was excruciatingly hard at times, but I knew in my heart of hearts that Christ was doing a long-awaited work in my life at a time I was ready to receive it. I felt Him very near through it all, and I spent lots of time in prayer through those hard days.

"I've always heard it said that the longest journey is the journey inward," she told us. "Honestly trying to look at what you are, what you have been, the mistakes you have made—well, it's terrifying, and so very humbling. Shame and guilt rush in like a flood at times, especially in the areas where you feel you have failed your children. At the same time, I considered it a wonderful opportunity and a great privilege—a chance to know myself better, to change and to grow. I had nothing to lose except pride.

"So first of all I asked the Holy Spirit to guide my words through it all, and to help me to do anything I could to help both of you experience more freedom in your lives. I asked Him to make our family a place where honesty and openness with each other was much easier than it had been. And I prayed that He would not let this time of working through the pain end before I was what and where He wanted me." She stopped and smiled at us. "I think it's called 'sanctification'—the Spirit chiseling away, making us more and more like Christ. Bless

Him, He just will not let us stay the same! At least, not comfortably."

~

Recently I had a good friend tell me, in tears, that her grown
daughter had done some soul-searching and had shared some
of the things she and her husband had done, unknowingly, that
had hurt her as a child. My friend was struggling with how to
respond. So many emotions flowed—many of them coming
from a desire to defend her parenting. I was able to tell her
about the response that my mother had courageously chosen—
and the healing that followed. My friend wrote back a few
weeks later, thanking me for the advice and telling me how
she'd seen incredible changes, for the better, in her relationship
with her daughter.

Since that time, my own grown children, along with Scott
and me, have been through a few counseling sessions. And this
time, *I* got a taste of what it is like to be the Mama under the
microscope and to hear the ways we'd caused our children
pain. Not easy. But to have the chance—to respond to our kids'
woundedness, to say how we much we loved them, how we
blew it, how immature we were at times—was also a blessed
privilege, and it took our relationship with them to new levels.

Henri Nouwen compared the maturing of our lives to the
sacrament of the communion bread: We are taken, broken,
blessed—and then given. Perhaps nowhere else is this process
more evident than within our all-too-human families. And
perhaps nowhere else is it as much worth the effort.

*Our fathers [and mothers] disciplined us for a little while
as they thought best; but God disciplines us for our good,
that we may share in his holiness.*

—Hebrews 12:10

Mom in Analysis

~

"Some aspects of the mother–daughter affection are forever a one-way street, because, unlike other attachments, your mother is always your mother, and you are always her child… I am reminded of a 50-year-old friend of mine who, in a voice heavy with concern, told me, 'My daughter phoned last night to say that yesterday was the worst day of her life: her boss bawled her out and her boyfriend broke up with her. So I went to her apartment with a care package of take-out Chinese food and flowers from my garden.

" 'Here's my question: *Am I infantilizing her?*'

"It is a question only a mother would ask. 'No,' I replied, shaking with laughter and more than a bit envious of her daughter. 'You're just being a mother—and a friend.' "

CHAPTER 24

Honor the Matriarch—
Your Turn Cometh!

~

Throughout the centuries it has usually been the daughters, mothers, grandmothers, and great-grandmothers who are the emotional heart of family genealogies. My husband's great-grandmother Peterson was the legendary Matriarch of Serenity and Goodness in the Freeman family tree. More than 25 years ago, when Scott and I first began dating, I heard epic tales from the Freeman family of their beloved Grandma Peterson.

She loved her Lord Jesus deeply and her family almost as well. She also adored cooking food—food so good you'd slap out your brains just licking your lips in anticipation. Just hearing stories of her scrumptious rye bread spread with homemade rhubarb jam made my mouth water.

Not long before Great-Grandmother Peterson died at age 93, my new father-in-law, Jim, took me on a long trip to meet his beloved grandmother. Scott and his sister, Laura, made the trip also.

Grandma lived in a quaint older home near where her Swedish husband had made a living from the family farm. I immediately thought of the hearty immigrants from Sweden in Willa Cather's novel *O Pioneers!*

By the time of our visit, Grandma Peterson was just a wisp of a woman—sitting in her rocker, her tiny lap covered with an old shawl. By the soft glow of a nearby lamp, Scott and I talked with her. I knew that Grandma Peterson's only daughter, Irene, had died at 28, leaving behind two small boys—one of which was Jim, my new father-in-law. There had been great affection between Grandma Peterson and Irene. Only after Jim was a grown man did he learn that his mother was not Grandma Peterson's daughter by blood. It had simply never crossed Grandma Peterson's mind to tell her grandson otherwise. Irene was Grandma Peterson's child through love—which was, in this case, much thicker than blood. As our conversation warmed, I asked Grandma Peterson how she had lived through losing her daughter 40 years before.

When I leaned close to hear her answer, I noticed two tears suspended on the edge of her soft, ancient eyelids.

"Honey, it was the hardest thing I ever went through," she said softly. "And I hurt so bad for little Jim and Lee, left without their mama. But—with the Lord's help, life goes on." She paused, then added, "Not a day goes by I don't think of Irene, and I'm looking forward to heaven, when I'll see her again."

It was then I realized that, although Grandma Peterson had managed to live a full and loving life, thoughts of her Irene still brought fresh feelings of loss, pain, and love. She epitomized the expression, "There's nothing stronger than a mother's love."

I instinctively reached for her frail hand. She squeezed my fingers tightly—a wordless gesture of compassion between two generations of women with nothing—and everything—in common. As our hands and hearts connected, I could almost feel myself, a supple young twig, being grafted onto the sturdy

Scandinavian branches of my husband's family tree. And I realized that it is probably the love, prayers, and encouragement of mothers like Grandma Peterson that has supplied the lifeblood for those family trees that blossom and flourish over the centuries.

That day when I sat holding Grandma Peterson's withered hand in my own young girl's hands, I could not imagine— could not think—that it would ever be possible to be as old as this frail woman. Yet, here I am, out of babies and just over the brink of grandmotherdom. I'm beginning to suspect how quickly the years pass. And I can see that someday I will be The Matriarch. For the first 18 years of my life, I was dependent on my mother. We are now both enjoying our individual independence, but isn't it strange how short a span of time it is before mother becomes dependent on child? How deeply intertwined our lives are? How crucial to be at peace with one another?

As yet, my own mother is still vigorous, but I feel her passing the torch to me. She has cared for me. Someday I and my siblings will care for her. And someday, Rachel Praise and her brothers will care for me. And all of the painful ways we failed one another will be forgotten.

Mother and I have come to at least one conclusion as a result of writing down our experiences as adult children and as fairly functional parents. We've just about decided that we don't get perfect in this life in anything. The best we can hope for is Better, Much Better, or Mostly Wonderful. Most often, the path to Better is to forgive, love, and accept ourselves and our family members as we are (and some of us are very peculiar people).

Often, to our surprise, forgiveness opens the way for change that leads to Much Better, because we find that we have given the Spirit of God our permission to start the process of changing us. In other words, as we allow the Spirit to nourish us, we begin to see that we are being transformed into His like-ness. Then the fruit begins to grow—fruits of love, joy, peace, patience, kindness, gentleness—and we may soon find that life has become Mostly Wonderful. And somewhere, deep inside ourselves, we begin to recognize the faintest image of yet another Matriarch of Serenity and Goodness emerging to adorn our family's tree.

Your beauty…should be that of your inner self, the unfading beauty of a gentle and quiet spirit, which is of great worth in God's sight. For this is the way the holy women of the past who put their hope in God used to make themselves beautiful.

—1 Peter 3:3-5

CHAPTER 25

Shared Joy Is Double Joy

My children are growing up so fast! Recently a shy young man we have come to love made an appointment with Rachel's dad—yes, to ask for her hand in marriage. My shy little violet—beginning her lifelong journey on her way to Serenity and Goodness! It seems that only yesterday we were worrying about whether she would ever be persuaded to say a word when she got to first grade. Like a lot of things we worry about with our kids, we could have saved ourselves the trouble.

By the time first grade arrived, Rachel went off to school without protest and, to our great relief, soon began to speak when called upon by her teachers. By the time she reached fifth grade, her teachers told me she was actually volunteering answers and speaking right up in the classroom. However, she was still considered to be a quiet young lady in public, one who was serious about her work. At home, however, she was learning to boss her brothers around and express herself—sometimes all too well—to her father and me.

Fast-forward to age ten. I am having lunch with my strawberry-blonde daughter, who, at this delightful age, has the perfect sprinkling of both freckles and giggles. There are few silent moments. She takes wonderful care of her mother, reminding me in one restaurant not to leave my purse under the table, and in another not to go off without my purchase. She still has that penchant for doing things right that caused her to blurt forth her first words to her daddy years ago. When I have to return to various stores because I keep leaving things like my sunglasses and my organizer (ha!) notebook, Rachel just shakes her head and grins.

Now, turn the pages of her life very quickly. In June, she will walk down the aisle to marry handsome, soft-spoken Jody Rhodes—the shadowy figure I've wondered about all these years, the man who would be my daughter's husband. With a smile and easy manner that would put Brad Pitt to shame, this young man has not only won Rachel's heart but the hearts of our whole family.

My daughter is a unique blend. She's certainly got her share of her Granny's spunk and sassiness, which is not without its charm. (Both Scott and my daddy insist they like their women a little on the sassy side.) By God's grace and mercy, she has inherited her daddy's long legs, and he's the only one in the family who could possibly be responsible for her strong, silent genes. She shares her mother's passion for reading and shopping—and she definitely shares my ability to look, in the early mornings, like an alien with Don King hair.

But just as I've realized that Mother and I are not a carbon-copy, twin pair of turtledoves, and just as I've had to discover for myself exactly where it is I want to soar, Rachel too is about the business of finding her own unique place in the sun. That's fine with me, as long as she remembers to put on her clothes before she flies out the front door to go calling on the neighbors.

I hope (and trust) that, after she's married, we'll keep doing lunch. Not only so she can help me keep track of my belongings, but because I want the continued joy of watching her spread her one-of-a-kind wings.

Though finding our individuality and separateness from our moms is an essential part of the path to adulthood, I have found that there are moments when a mother is simply indispensable. Those moments fall into the following categories: 1) an intensely joyful occasion, such as a wedding day or the birth of a child, 2) a time of terrible disappointment or sorrow—such as when you've lost your best friend or a job you desperately wanted, and 3) an in-between, boring sort of day when there's nothing much going on at all.

On that in-between kind of day, you call your mom to chat about the excessive number of strings in the celery you bought that morning, or how you suddenly got tickled when you noticed that the seed wart on your index finger looked like a little old man sporting a bad toupee. And I'll be expecting equally profound calls from Mrs. Jody Rhodes.

When I think of my mother's encouragement over the years (not to mention the sheer fun we've had together), a variety of scenes flip through my mind. I see myself at age 11, crying in her arms about all the kids at school who weren't standing in line to be my friend. Going forward in time, I see her touching the edge of my wedding veil and telling me I'm the most beautiful bride she's ever seen. I hear her voice at the birth of my first son—saying, above the most excruciating pain I have ever felt, "You're my hero, Becky. You can do this!" And I remember her comments as I handed her the first rough draft of a story about a crazy day with three-year-old Gabriel.

"Becky," she said, "you've got the gift. With a little help, you can get this published." Mother provided the help I needed, and after three years of writing, praying, editing, rejection, close calls, hair-pulling, and trying again, our first book—*Worms in My Tea*—found a home.

Upon hearing the good news from the publisher, I searched all over town for just the right card to send Mother to let her know how much she meant to me in helping to make another dream come true. Then I found it—the perfect card. On the front was a picture of two beautiful black-and-white whales (I'm sure they were mother and daughter) leaping together from the foam of the bright blue ocean toward an equally blue sky. I knew Mother had seen *Free Willy* three times, and she knew I had always been fascinated by whales. Across the bottom of the card was written an old Swedish proverb:

"Shared joy is double joy, and shared sorrow is half-sorrow."

Perhaps the saying originated with one of Scott's relatives from the old country—perhaps from a young Scandinavian mother, her blonde braids pulled back in one of those fancy knots that look like a pretzel.

In my vision I see her in a long blue skirt under a freshly starched apron, its folds dancing in the breeze. She is sitting on a lush, green hill overlooking the North Sea, enjoying a picnic of cheese, crusty bread, and sweet goat's milk with her adorable daughter. The sun sends down a splash of light, just enough to illuminate the young daughter's flaxen hair, making her look almost angelic in the afternoon breeze. (Yes, I've been told I have a vivid imagination.)

Suddenly, out in the ocean, two magnificent creatures leap in unison toward the sky. Mother and child observe the miracle together from the shore. Then the awe-inspired mother blinks hard, swallows deeply, reaches across the picnic blanket, and covers her little girl's hand with her own. Gazing into her daughter's deep blue eyes, the Swedish mother utters a timeless pearl that will someday be written on a perfect card beneath a picture of two black-and-white whales. The card will find its way to an American department store, and finally, a daughter named Becky will buy it for her mother, whose name is Ruthie. The card's message reads, "Shared joy is double joy, and shared sorrow is half-sorrow."

Then someday, Becky will pass the saying on to her daughter, Rachel Praise, who will share it with her daughter and her daughter's daughter. And so on it will go as long as there are generations of mothers and daughters who experience the doubled delight of discovering that they are becoming more than just mother and daughter. They are becoming very good friends.

Your mother was like a vine in your vineyard
planted by the water; it was fruitful and
full of branches because of abundant water.

—Ezekiel 19:10

Postlude:

Becoming Buds with Our Grown-Up Babies

Becoming Buds with Our Grown-Up Babies

A Final Word from Ruthie

I wonder how many mothers who read the above title are tempted to shout, "Yes! That's what I want. But why is it that every time I open my mouth, I step on her toes?" If it's any consolation—this, too, shall probably pass. And it will probably come back again. So much depends on what phase one or the other of us is in. And yes, we mothers still have our "phases," too. Just ask my older daughter, Becky, and my younger daughter, Rachel, who is just as much fun as Becky. Amazing.

But back to our discussion of phases. For our daughter, there's the heavenly Little-Girl Phase, when she thinks we really know what we're doing, even though we may not seem like a best friend to her while we're doing it. Then there's the Teenage Phase, when she often doubts we know anything about anything, but who else is awake to talk to when she comes in from a date? Then there's the Young-Adult Phase, when she thinks we actually knew what we were doing when we did all those things that have warped her so terribly. Once we get through that, usually we enjoy a period of time when we are Best Friends—and we both feel that way.

About this time Daughter has gotten married and has had a child of her own, and suddenly she discovers how hard it is to be a mom. We grandmothers are in our heyday! They NEED us (with a capital N), and at last—at last—they understand! This lovely Sisters-Under-the-Skin Phase lasts until we begin to feel that our grandchild needs more discipline (or less), or our daughter feels like we feel that way. Or we ever so tactfully let her know that you can get at that little line of dirt around the stove burners with a good stiff toothbrush. (You can just imagine how that plays with today's hysterically busy mother. She may have visions of just how that toothbrush would look tied in a bowknot around our neck.)

Whatever opinions we may have about whatever (and there are lots of them by this stage in life), she usually knows what they are. Yet here she is, trying her best to make her own life and home her way, and all day long she hears the echo of our voice from the years past telling her how we would do it if we were her. This is clearly the "Please, Mother, I'd Rather Do It Myself!" stage. And then we call, with the best of intentions, and offer to help her redecorate. It's really not too hard to see how, at this stage, every time we open our mouths we step on her toes, is it?

But again, we pass through this phase, and she has learned to manage life just the way she wants to, and she's doing great at it. Now it's our turn to feel insecure. She knows how to use the Internet. She drives the freeway, fearless. She can make her own travel reservations and go to strange cities and find her way to hotels, laughing at any misadventures along the way. Hard as it is to face, she knows how to manage today's world better than we do!

Mixed in with our pride in her and our gratitude to God that she is doing so well, we experience a twinge of sadness as we realize our babies are now running the world. Soon they will have to manage us. (I have it in writing from Becky that "when you get senile I promise to make sure your socks always match." What concerns me most is that she may forget where she put me.) For a lot of us, it's hard to give up the driver's seat. Somehow, we just didn't expect it, at least not so soon. But we'll get over it!

I've been a mom for more than 40 years now, and a daughter for 60. I've passed through most of the phases of being both. I've cared for my own beloved, senile mother and seen her off to be with Jesus. During that time of caring for her, I experienced almost every emotion that it's possible for womankind to feel. I felt moments of deep compassion, rending love, exquisite frustration, and amazing irritation.

I know how hard it can be to graduate from this life to the next, and how desperately we need our children and their love at the end of life—about as much as they needed us and our love at the beginning of theirs. How can we expect that—through such a changing, intense relationship—we will always feel like the best of buddies? But with the help of God's sweet Spirit, we can actually be our daughter's best friend, whether or not either of us feels it at all times. I offer these five tips from a number that I've gleaned from some successes and many failures.

Center Your Heart in Rearing Your Children

By 1965, the feminist messages were beginning to seep into women's magazines, and one of them was this: "It's a mistake to make raising your family your whole life. You should be more than just an extension of your husband and children."

So I went out into the community and worked in some causes, joined some clubs, and became president of one or two. Soon I was nominated for Outstanding Young Woman of the Year, and on the day of the award luncheon, my world changed forever. I didn't win, but I sat there listening to the list of accomplishments of the woman who did. The list was as long as my arm. At the end, the reader finished triumphantly, "And with all this, she manages to be the mother of two small children!"

The scene before me faded, the voice grew distant. A recent scene flashed before me. It was of my son, David, telling me about his day at school, and I suddenly realized something— he had been holding onto my skirt to keep me there until he finished.

Suddenly I wanted to cry. I wanted out of that gathering— I wanted to be home and fully available to my children. It was what I wanted to do with my life, and I have never for one moment regretted it. The nearer I get to my own Graduation Day from this life, the more I realize that it's the relationships in life that matter, not the accomplishments.

Have Lots of Fun

There's an old saw that's been around a long time, but early on it was enormously helpful to me. It is, "Treat your guests like family, and your family like guests." To me, this meant that my guests should feel free to take off their shoes and prop their feet up on our old coffee table. As for treating my family like guests, I tried always to give each of them a warm welcome when they came home, to spend time chatting with them, to listen to what they had to say with respect, and to pay attention to their "knock-knock jokes" until my eyes glazed over and my mouth felt frozen in a grotesque smile.

Treating my family like guests also meant planning moments and events that were just for fun. A favorite was to wait until Sunday afternoon to make dessert, and then gather each family member to the table and serve dessert so we could laugh and talk together—just like guests invited over for pie and coffee.

In our family we sang together, we danced together, we played table games together, and as the children grew into their teen years, we discussed the books of men like Francis Schaeffer with them, often along with college students from church. On many a Saturday night around midnight, the discussion would degenerate, and we would wind up rolling on the floor with laughter. As I remember it, we had lots of fun.

Dare to Discipline

To a child, being required to do the hard thing seems anything but friendly, but a parent who does not realize that rearing a child means constant training of that child is not being a true friend to her child. All too often, the child has a feeling of insecurity, as if no one cared enough to require her to do what she knows, deep in her heart, she should do. In extreme cases, children develop a slow-burning anger and contempt toward the parent who doesn't care enough to discipline.

And Then…Don't Dare to Discipline

There comes a time when (let us hope!) our job is over. They're off our payroll, as my husband is terribly fond of saying. (This is said with a gleeful little jig.) The time for training from us is past. We mustn't try to tactfully sneak in little hints—they will know. What they now most need is our encouragement and affirmation, and the need for that never goes away. I know men and women in their 60s who are still grieving because one parent or the other never seemed to approve of them, or never told them outright that they loved them.

Listen Carefully to the Criticisms of Your Adult Children

They just might be right. When Rachel found the courage to write The Letter to her dad and me (see the story in chapter 23), she gave us a precious gift. Even with all the pain that came with it, there was a fabulous opportunity to understand something of what had been going on inside Rachel's heart and mind over the years. (Don't most of us sometimes ask ourselves, *What is going on in that young'un's mind right now? What does she think of me as a parent?*) After that, I at least knew some of the thoughts and reactions she had had in that long-ago time when she was a little girl—before that little girl vanished and became a young woman.

Best of all, during this long segment of our Family Journey Inward, our daughters graciously gave us a chance to make some things right—and to go on from that point in our lives to greater closeness and joy in one another as a family. Today, I sometimes feel like pinching myself to have been so blessed! Certainly I feel like hugging them around the neck when I think of it.

Having said all that, I would offer a word of caution if you are an adult daughter thinking of writing such a letter to your mother or father or both of them. Remember that I had been asking for this kind of input for a long time. I suggest you pray long and hard about it, and then if you decide to go ahead, please, please be very tactful and kind. Begin with the good memories and express your love at the outset. And finally, you may want to have a professional counselor or a wise mentor read your letter first.

~

So. What does it really mean to be our daughter's adult friend? I don't think it necessarily means most intimate friend. I adored my own mother, yet there were things I told my sister and my friends that I did not tell her. But there were times when I was a young mother that only my mother could meet the ache and the need in my heart. I remember particularly the times when our babies were born—she came like a sweet, agreeable, ministering angel and made those days into Golden Memories as we enjoyed each new baby together.

One of the things I have most wanted for my daughters is that they would have a group of close friends—perhaps that one special friend who is at the same point in her life that Becky or Rachel has reached. I've also been delighted that they each have, or have had, an older woman friend–mentor who lives near them and is available for them, because they often can accept counsel from another older woman friend much better than they can from Mom.

But daughters and moms have a wonderfully unique relationship. Friendship is part of it, but far above friendship, we are Family. Ideally as such, we are deeply loved and cherished, each by the other, forever. If we've been blessed to have a daughter, God has given us a priceless gift. I suspect that all our lives, at various times, our relationship with our daughters will be a work in progress—but what a rewarding work it is.

Because we have lived longer than they have, we should be wiser. We can be willing to truly hear them and to change where we need to change. May we always pray for the maturity that allows us to forbear—as our daughters struggle to find their own way just as we struggled. And most important of all, our prayers can continually undergird their lives and make all the difference.

In short, being our daughters' good friends as adults is being willing to mirror the kind of friendship Jesus extends to us. It's always wanting and praying for what is truly best for them. Enjoy!

Notes

~

Unless otherwise noted, the source of all quotations is the Internet.

A Pair of Chocolate Nuts
Page 14: "My mother influences my choices…" Victoria Secunda, *When You and Your Mother Can't Be Friends: Resolving the Most Complicated Relationship of Your Life* (New York: Delta Publishing, 1991).

Chapter 1—Fowl Play
Page 21: "bunch of us were dizzily swaying…" Jeanmarie Coogan, "My Mother Barked Like a Seal," *Reader's Digest*, May 1994.

Chapter 3—Sick Little Chicks
Page 36: "For some people the memory…" Edith Schaeffer, *What Is a Family?* (Old Tappan, NJ: Fleming H. Revell, 1975), p. 102.

Chapter 4—We Rose and Called Her Blessed
Page 37: "I can do all things…" Philippians 4:13 KJV.

Page 40: "When peace like a river…" Hymn "It Is Well with My Soul," words by Horatio G. Spafford.

Chapter 10—Not My Mother's Thanksgiving
Page 75: "Minimize distorted perception…" Adapted from Joseph Michelli, *Humor, Play & Laughter: Stress-Proofing Life with Your Kids* (Golden, CO: Love & Logic Institute, Inc., 1998).

Chapter 11—Feathering Our Messy Nests with Memories
Pages 82-83: "When a flare of temper…"; "When some new little family…"; "Someone in the family…" Edith Schaeffer, *What Is a Family?* (Old Tappan, NJ: Fleming H. Revell, 1975), pp. 203, 205, 191.

Chapter 12—Irregular Relatives
Page 91: "Learning to handle hurts..." Fred Luskin, *Forgive for Good* (San Francisco: HarperSanFrancisco, 2002), p. 8-9.

A Positive Mom...
Pages 115-18: Adapted from "A Positive Mom..." Becky Freeman, "A Positive Mom...," *Becoming Family* magazine, 2001, Copyright © 2001 by Becky Freeman.

Chapter 16—Love Me, Love My Kids
Page 123: "Every time we get..." Terri Apter, Ruthellen Josselson, *Best Friends: The Pleasures and Perils of Girls' and Women's Friendships* (New York: Three Rivers Press, 1998).

Chapter 18—Lizards in My Living Room
Page 137: "The fine irony..." Paula Rinehart, *The Cleavers Don't Live Here Anymore* (Chicago: Moody Press, 1993), p. 47.
Page 140: "When you're following..." Martha Beck, *Finding Your Own North Star* (New York: Three Rivers Press, 2001), p. 52.

Chapter 20—Motherhood Means Never Having to Say, "I'm Organized"
Page 147: "When we were children..." Becky Freeman and Ruthie Arnold, *Worms in My Tea: and Other Mixed Blessings* (Nashville, TN: Broadman & Holman Publishers, 1994), p. 11.
Page 149: "As memories..."; "went into labor after..." Freeman and Arnold, p. 16.
Page 150: "I fully expect that..." Freeman and Arnold, p. 17.

Chapter 23—We're All Grown-Ups Here—Finally!
Page 169: "Some aspects of..." Victoria Secunda, *When You and Your Mother Can't Be Friends: Resolving the Most Complicated Relationship of Your Life* (New York: Delta Publishing, 1991).

Becoming Buds with Our Grown-Up Babies
Pages 183-89: "Becoming Buds with..." Adapted from Ruthie Arnold, "How to Be Your Daughter's Best Friend," *HomeLife* magazine, May 1998. Copyright © 1998 Ruthie Arnold.

Other Books by Becky

Chocolate Chili Pepper Love
Coffee Cup Friendship & Cheesecake Fun
Lemonade Laughter & Laid-Back Joy
Milk & Cookies to Make You Smile
Peanut Butter Kisses & Mud Pie Hugs
Real Magnolias
Worms in My Tea

For Kids

Camp Wanna Banana Mysteries
Gabe & Critters Series

Drop by for a visit at Becky's virtual "porch swing"
www.beckyfreeman.com
While there, check out the Becky Bags!